THE

th🔘ught leaders

PRACTICE

Matt Church
Peter Cook
Scott Stein

Published by Thought Leaders Publishing

Thought Leaders Publishing
Suite 8, Rear 510 Sydney Road
Balgowlah NSW 2093

First published 2012 as *Sell Your Thoughts*
HarperCollinsPublishers (New Zealand) Limited
P.O. Box 1, Auckland 1140

Matt Church, Peter Cook and Scott Stein assert the moral right to be identified as the authors of this work.

ISBN: 978 0 9775724 9 6

Design & typesetting by Michael Fink

Contents

Preface

Welcome to *The Thought Leaders Practice*! For more than 15 years we have been teaching people how to capture, package and deliver their ideas in a way that is commercially smart. Now, in this book, we will share with you the tried and tested methodologies that have helped thousands of information experts make a difference in the lives of those people and businesses they interact with, and get paid accordingly. This book was first published by Harper Collins as *Sell Your Thoughts* in 2011. We've learned a lot since then, and this edition comes with the benefit of those lessons, along with a new title.

With the success of the Thought Leaders Business School program we are super clear that we teach experts how to bill $500,000–$1,500,000 working 50-200 days a year with one or maybe two staff. We are also super clear that this labor of love needs to be run lightly with a scoreboard much like any game. We know that clever people have a tendency to sabotage their commercial success in all kinds of clever ways. This process and the focus of this book is to help you circumvent these self sabotaging behaviors (most of them unconscious) and put you well on your way to success as a thought leader in a practice.

In essence, what we will show you is how to generate a highly leveraged income as a subject-matter expert. We want to show you an alternative model to the two traditional choices of *get a job* or *run a business*. Although the tax-collecting authorities will consider you a business, and while you need to accept this as a mechanical fact, we are going to suggest that you operate with the mindset of a specialist or practitioner. We are inviting you to consider running your own thought leadership practice based on your expertise — to make a living by selling your thoughts, to make it a game that gives you the chance to do work you love, with people you like the way you want.

Our three wishes

We have three wishes for this book (and if you are going to have wishes, three is the right number to have). One is for the world, one is for you, and one is a selfish wish for us.

Our wish for the world is that you get to make the contribution that you were born to make. That you get to make a difference to thousands or even millions of people through your practice. That your books, your speeches, your programs, your coaching and your ideas touch lives all over the planet. That by selling your thoughts you leave the world better than you found it.

Our wish for you is that you live your dream as you are making that difference. That you get very well paid to do work you love, with people you like, the way you want. However that looks for you. That you get to truly create your life.

Our final wish is for us. Our vision is to be part of a meme pool of a thousand thought leaders. We imagine an event where a thousand well-resourced, clever people who have been through this journey are coming together to explore how to work together for the betterment of all. Think of all the problems that we would solve, the projects we would create and the contributions we would make! We would love you to be part of that.

Acknowledgements

Blending over 60 years of insights into a book does not occur overnight. This book brings together the ideas that we have used, experienced, taught and lived with, in our own practices as well as with countless others. In addition, with three authors who travel to work with clients all over the globe, it has taken a true team effort. Without the encouragement of numerous people, this book would have remained an idea in our heads, rather than a resource for others to use.

On a personal level, Matt thanks Pete and Scott for working tirelessly to make this the best book possible. As always, Matt is grateful for his gorgeous family, Lexie, Nicholas and Chloe, who make everything more colourful and worthwhile; his amazing support team for years of unflagging support and extraordinary efforts in a high-end, full-on thought leaders practice; Ivan for his equally amazing tenure and support in all things life based. A huge thanks to the thought leaders partner and mentor community and every graduate of the thought leaders business school program.

Pete would like to thank his beautiful wife, Trish. His thanks are for continuing to believe in him when he gave you reason to doubt, being his partner when he needed it most, sticking with him when times were tough, and sharing this magnificent adventure with him. He couldn't have done it without you. To his brothers in arms, Matt and Scott: it is an absolute honour and privilege to work with you and partner you both. And, finally, to his clients past and present: thank you for backing him, trusting him and paying him — you are an integral part of his journey and this book.

Scott specifically wants to thank his family, Natalie, Jasmine, Isabella and Luca, for being such a great inspiration and support. He would also like to thank both his parents, Larry and Lorene Stein, for raising him to believe that he could do anything he set his mind to and for all the encouragement along the way. He hopes he can pass on this wonderful upbringing to his kids! Finally, Scott would like to thank Matt for his amazing foresight, vision and friendship, and Pete for his conviction in taking the thought leaders program to the next level — both of you rock!

We would also like to thank each of the case study black belts, including: Michael Henderson for being a leader by example in the Thought Leaders tribe; Sean Richardson and Darren Hill for sharing their amazing ideas and model on wealth mindsets and their gracious story of becoming black belts; Rowdy McClean for demonstrating how to 'Get Real' and make things happen; Domonique Bertolucci for showing how to transition from a high- flying corporate career to a successful practice; Avril Henry for sharing her insights in shifting from HR to Leadership — and challenging a male-dominated military tradition; and Peter Sheahan for demonstrating his unique journey and impact on multiple hemispheres. Their willingness to share their experiences so that others may benefit is humbling.

We also have had wonderful support and ideas for this book from visionary thought leaders, including Geoff McDonald for his contribution as the 'games guru'; Debbie Roberts for her inspiring example of becoming a thought leader with a market as small as Australian bookkeepers and the grace, humility and wisdom with which she shared her journey; Jenny Vickers for her legal insight and wisdom; Neen James and Mel Abraham for helping us to spread the word in the United States and being amazing ambassadors for Thought Leaders; and Neville Cook for reviewing this book with the same thoroughness, wisdom and love with which he has been proofreading Pete's writing for the last 25 years.

And finally to you, the reader. We thank you for taking the time to broaden your ideas and potential, to begin your journey to sell your ideas and increase your impact in all areas of your life.

Matt, Pete and Scott

Introduction

A marketplace of sameness

The business landscape is changing, and fast-growth enterprises are jumping ahead of the pack, marketing with personality and running their businesses with ingenuity. Currently there is a great 'blanding' in the marketplace as traditional companies sell 'same same' products and services as each other, trying to compete on price. This is a foolish game. Only the biggest businesses with the greatest purchasing power and seemingly infinite capital reserves can compete by offering the lowest price. New players, start-ups and businesses on the edge of re-invention need to explore the innovation fringe. They need to come up with ideas that change the game. A great example of this is what Facebook did to Myspace. In 2008 Myspace had 300 million users and was purchased by Rupert Murdoch's Newscorp for US$580 million. By 2011 Facebook had not only grown to almost 800 million users, but it was also championing the new marketing segment of social media. And the result for Myspace? Murdoch sold it in July 2011 for US$39 million. To survive in this new environment, leaders will need to evolve their businesses faster than the pace of change. They need to be thought leaders.

Competitive advantage will lie at the edge of market opportunity with unknown innovations. Twenty-five years ago, Richard Saul Wurman (one of the world's first acknowledged futurists) and a few colleagues anticipated that three industries were going to collide. These industries — technology, entertainment and design — form the acronym TED. The viral popularity of the resulting TED.com website, which has thousands of the world's leading thinkers sharing their ideas openly and freely for all, is a platform for thought leadership. The way the TED 'organization' operates is thought-leading. TED creates a space where the public's desire to participate in mind-opening, paradigm-shifting conversations occurs. People are not only open to new ideas, they are craving them. You only need look at the rise of retail superstar Apple this decade — and how the blend of technology, entertainment and design in their products proves Wurman's foresight to be prophetic. That's thought leadership!

Old challenges — new thinking ... in action

Whether it's generating fresh drinking water in Africa or re-inventing collapsed industries in Detroit, we need new thinking to help solve established problems. Consider the list of challenges that people face socially, politically or commercially, and you begin to see the need — no, more than that, the *imperative* — for thinking at new levels. This goes far beyond simple creativity or even product innovation. It goes to the heart of human endeavour, the future of the planet and the role we, the human race, play in that future. As Einstein said, 'The problems that exist in the world today cannot be solved by the level of thinking that created them.' An exciting tomorrow will be created by thought leaders.

However, it's not just thinking that will affect things; it's the quality of the action around that thinking. We define thought leadership as 'thinking in action'. We choose to organize our conversations around a commercial agenda. Having a customer who values your idea enough to buy it is the fastest way we know to measure the quality of the idea.

Business is not a force for good in its own right. In fact, there are plenty of companies that have sacrificed their services, products, employees, the environment and their community for short-term profits. However, we believe the central idea of business is a worthy one — be successful by creating value for others. If you organize your ideas in such a way that others will pay for them, you just might be onto something.

Money alone does not make an idea worthy; many of the world's best ideas have no commercial application. But generally it's going to be easier to implement these ideas if you are well resourced. We believe that a committed group of thought leaders can take these worthy ideas and put them into practice. That is why we help clever people be commercially smart.

A shift in information sharing

As will.i.am from the Black Eyed Peas says, 'When Google is your professor and Wikipedia is your encyclopedia, you can become a kitchen expert in almost anything. The problem with kitchen experts is that they don't always have the wisdom to know the difference between good and bad information. This is where subject-matter experts come in. We need someone who can help us sift the information we discover and help make it relevant to our world. Thought leaders are, at their core, meaning makers.

Today you can book flights to and accommodation in almost any country in the world, online, yourself. If you have recently been on a family vacation, you will have explored the location of the hotel on Google Maps using Street View, checked out the hotel's guest comments on tripadvisor.com and been pretty well-informed about what it costs, where to go and what to ask for when you get there. However, many people still want an expert who has been there and will share their insights — and many travel agents are using this angle to survive in their rapidly changing industry. Some are becoming leaders on Trip Advisor with followers in the tens of thousands.

We have moved our need from *information knowledge* to *applied wisdom*; from *expert* to *trusted authority*. It's this shift that information experts need to understand. A PhD used to mean that you had very deep knowledge in a narrow field — you were the expert in your field. This is no longer enough; the information is now available to us all, it's the ability to draw meaning and application that is a higher value. It's at this exact distinction that you start to take what you know and make it more valuable to others. You go from knowing stuff to being known for knowing stuff. You go from having the answers to being able to create the need.

Most of us need to know more about how that information will make a difference in the lives of others — without it being lost in a university classroom with students not listening as they distract themselves on Instagram or Facebook. Knowledge is not a competitive advantage — knowing *how* to apply that knowledge to achieve a specific, desired outcome is!

A trusted authority

Thought leader on marketing and bestselling author Seth Godin talks often and voraciously about the need to stand out and be remarkable. He explores themes of building trusted communities and communicating with them in an attractive, respectful and permission-based way.

Chris Anderson, the editor in chief of *Wired* magazine, explores the shifting landscape of information access. He makes the comment that information is no longer scarce, and, in a world where it's now freely available, there is a shift away from informational control and charging for access to it. The idea of value around information is shifting. You need to know more than the obvious answer to any given questions. You need to be able to create new insights and repurpose old insights so that they are relevant. This is thought leadership.

The different games you could play

Thought Leaders Global is an educational organization that focuses on growing practices, businesses and careers. In this book we set out to tell our story and share the strategy we use to build a 'specialist infopreneurial' practice (we'll explain this term in a little while if it is new to you). It is worth understanding the game we are choosing to play in this book. It's not the only game in town; we don't even go so far as to say it's the best game in town (although it is). It is simply a different game to the ones most people play.

The career game — Get a job!

When you leave school or college you typically get a job, learn some skills and spend 40–50 hours or so a week using those skills as part of someone else's business. This is a typical path for most of the working population.

After a while, if you apply yourself, you rise up through the ranks, get really good at what you know, and maybe even find some ways to contribute to the workings of your organization. Many thought leaders we meet love the challenge of large companies — they love innovating and running large-scale projects within big businesses and organizations. These people who work for someone else can still be thought leaders — they simply do their great work within businesses. They are what we call 'intrapreneurs'.

This book is not about getting a job.

The business game — Run your own company

Many people decide that they want the freedom of working for themselves and so they start a business. This can occur when they realize that they are working to benefit someone else, or that they want to be in control of their own destiny. Many simply become 'business owners' who have in effect bought themselves a job, working within the business they create — often up to 60–70 hours per week! Some, however, work on their businesses and go on to become 'entrepreneurs' as they look for ways to start, grow and exit a business. The thrill of building businesses and selling them for lottery-like figures is the game they are playing.

This book is not about starting, building and selling a business. And it's definitely not about buying a job.

The practice game — Sell your thoughts

We believe that a specialist can achieve an income approaching and even exceeding $1,000,000 a year by leveraging their expertise and employing maybe one or two personal assistants. The infopreneur (a one-person business, such as an independent consultant) is a relatively new category of worker. Fiercely independent, unconventional, non-traditional and growing in numbers, these people search for greater freedom and more control over their destiny.

The following model, the Thought Leaders Revenue Ladder, illustrates the income levels many of our program graduates have achieved. This 'white belt to black belt' model is the key focus of this book and your thoughts leaders practice game. We will expand further on this model later on and give you specific strategies that you can use to move through these levels.

BELT	INCOME	FOCUS
5th Dan	$1,200,000	Distribution
4th Dan	$1,080,000	Capacity
3rd Dan	$960,000	Productivity
2nd Dan	$840,000	Engagement
Black Belt	$720,000	Investment
Red Belt	$600,000	Leverage
Blue Belt	$480,000	Positioning
Green Belt	$360,000	Activity
Yellow Belt	$240,000	Value
White Belt	$120,000	Decision

Who will say we are wrong?

Business experts will suggest that you are running an income-based practice and that if you don't work, you won't earn money. We know this, and are quite intentional about building the whole 'practice' model around one income-generating guru. This is not for everyone. You have to be an expert, love what you do and want to actively put yourself out there 50–200 days a year (and just to be clear, it will start at 200). The game is to get paid extremely well doing work you love, with people you like, the way you want.

How do you become an 'infopreneur'?

The word infopreneur is a hybrid one that combines 'information' and 'entrepreneur'. This term has come to be commonplace in the world of information marketing, but its definition is still a bit vague. For us, it is someone who sells their ideas and expertise, or their intellectual property (IP), in a way that others value.

Infopreneurs become recognized as thought leaders when they clearly define a unique perspective or offering to the market based around the subject they are an expert in — when they build on the existing thinking in their field.

Success in our world is an infopreneur who has successfully commercialized his or her thought leadership and is running a practice that is turning over a million dollars or more a year with one or two support staff. Most people think this is impossible: 'Make a seven-figure income selling my expertise — are you serious?'

This is the game we are choosing to play in this book — the game of building a million-dollar practice selling your thoughts. So this book will help you if:

1. You have a specialist knowledge that you know could be used more effectively.

2. You are happy to rely on your own personal exertions to get ahead (i.e. you're not afraid of rolling up your sleeves and getting to work).

3. You want to do all this with a minimum of staffing or up-front capital investment.

We want to be very clear from the outset what this book is *not* going to do for you:

1. This book does not teach you how to build passive income — it teaches you how to build high income through *your* efforts!

2. This book does not teach you how to leverage the time of others — it teaches you how to leverage *your* time!

3. This book does not teach you how to build a business that you can sell — it teaches you how to create an income that will drive your investments, while you continue to do what you love.

Any idea you have can make you money if it is captured, packaged and delivered in a way other people value. In the book *Thought Leaders* we explain the rise in thought leadership and provide the nine essential skills that thought leaders demonstrate. In this book we will show you how to create your own commercial practice leveraging your thought leadership. If you become the recognized expert in your field, you can easily earn a high six-figure or seven-figure income, working 50–200 days a year with one or two support staff.

For people who may currently be an employee, this may require a move from being a subject-matter expert who *knows something* to becoming a trusted advisor who is *known for knowing something*.

As a subject-matter expert, you know something that others don't. Often, you are being asked to share that information with others. Maybe you are asked to speak. Perhaps someone suggests you write a book. It could be that people are always calling to pick your brain, buy you lunch or shout you a coffee. When we hear or see this happening, we know that this person has the potential to be a thought leader; they simply may not have recognized it yet.

The Thought Leaders programs and the ideas in this book illustrate the various stages of income and key activities you need to undertake to progress to the next level. The focus is on you running a practice (not a business) and using the six delivery modes of speaking, authoring, training, mentoring, facilitating and coaching to leverage what you know, to people who value it.

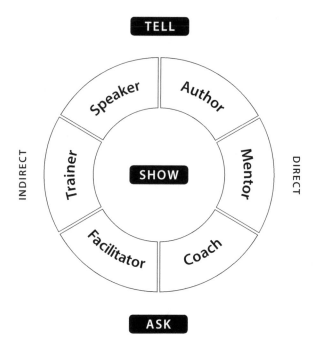

The journey to becoming a thought leader

Success in life is often achieved by choosing to ignore ultimatums and dogma and instead to get comfortable with paradox, ambiguity and contradiction. The examples we will share and the process we teach in this book is full of these. It's all about adaptable world views, about being able to shift perspective through unlearning things along the way.

When you are at point A, the world needs to be processed with A filters. When you are at point B, you need to shift away from point A and start to filter things with a point B perspective. Most people buy into the illusion that shifting perspectives is a linear process — just shifting shades of grey. What we want you to do is to be able to appreciate both viewpoints, and see how you can blend both into working together at the same time. Get comfortable with expanding your viewpoints, as this is the key to fast growth. You will need to stay open-minded, have courage and trust the system.

Each stage (or belt) you achieve in the Thought Leaders journey gives you new perspectives. As you get to each point, you make better choices.

No matter where you are currently placed on the revenue ladder and no matter when you get to read this book, you can create stability and a fantastic lifestyle by embracing infopreneurship. We believe that every soul is born with a message to share. We start by living and learning our message, and then when we start to teach it, we can truly get it.

So what are you waiting for? Become a thought leader and start on your path today. Make more money from selling the thoughts you have!

Read on, if you dare.

Business Model

1.

Practice vs Business

*Deciding what not to do is as important
as deciding what to do.*

— Steve Jobs

Mostly we think of two ways to earn an income — get a job or run a business. Of course when you get a job you are usually working in someone else's organization.

There is a third option that is often overlooked — a practice. This book is all about how to build a very specific type of practice — an 'infopreneurial' or thought leaders practice. We believe that for clever people who like to teach and share advice this is a very compelling model. But we're getting ahead of ourselves. Let's unpack the distinctions between a business and a practice.

WHAT'S A PRACTICE?

A practice is based on the expertise of the principal. Taking, for example, the case of brain surgery, the practice is based on the expertise of the surgeon. Whilst there are other people in the practice supporting her, the surgeon is the one who does all the delivery (in this case, the brain surgery). If she is sick, the receptionist isn't going to fill in for her. Without the brain surgeon, the practice isn't worth anything.

If you are a brain surgeon, you make money by performing surgery. You can't create a procedure manual for brain surgery and train an apprentice to take over while you sit on a beach somewhere. The whole practice is built around the expert — the brain surgeon. Everyone from the receptionist to the nurse is there to help the brain surgeon do her job, and to bring in the money.

The structure is a very hierarchical kind of a triangle. A practice runs top down — everything gets created and deployed from the principal's mind. A great team in the triangle is, of course, essential. The players in these practices are very much interdependent.

In the case of an infopreneurial practice, everything is built around the subject-matter expertise — or the ideas — of the principal. The expert is typically a consultant, speaker, author, trainer, mentor, facilitator or coach (and as we will see shortly, is ideally a combination of these).

Practices, compared with businesses, generally have low start-up costs and are then funded from the cash flow created in the practice. For example, you get a website when you can afford one. Businesses, on the other hand, have an initial investment focus (which may be a low-budget start-up) with later raising of funds or capital investment to get them to the next level. A practice needs to operate with low running costs and high margins. Because you can't sell a practice at the end, you need to be making good money along the way.

Unlike businesses, where owners seek to create systems and replace themselves, the practice owner never gets replaced. From day one, the job of the thought leader within the practice is to think, sell and deliver. Eventually there will be support staff to help do all the other things, but the principal will still be doing the thinking, selling and delivering. Consequently, to run a thought leader's practice you have to be prepared to work hard (especially at the start), and you have to love what you do.

WHAT'S A BUSINESS?

There are all sorts of businesses, from the Ford Motor Company down to your neighborhood restaurant or milk bar (for Gen Y readers — a milk bar is like a convenience store from the olden days that closes at night and doesn't sell frozen slushies).

A successful business can operate separately from its founder or owner and, if it's set up right, can be sold. It is essentially about leveraging something other than the owner to make money. It might be leveraging other people's time (staff) or it could be leveraging a technology or a piece of machinery. To be a business, you have to go from doing the work to getting the work done.

An unsuccessful business is one where the owner has bought themselves a job — and typically a low-paid job with long hours working for a lunatic (themselves). In his bestselling book *The E-Myth*, Michael Gerber explores what he calls the 'entrepreneurial seizure'. This is the moment when people decide to start their own business. He uses the seizure analogy because he believes many have that initial entrepreneurial spark, only to revert to working for a wage, but this time with the responsibility of paying all the bills as well.

Gerber's suggestion is that you should obsess about systems and procedures, and as a result leverage process to gain freedom for the owner. He suggests that you run every business like a turnkey franchise: systematize whatever you can so that the 'lowest common denominator' staff can operate with the highest level of efficiency.

Systems can definitely set you free. They don't only apply to businesses — they also apply to practices. However, there is an important distinction around the primary focus of the game of business versus the game of practice. It's about whether the focus is on *freedom* and money, or *fulfillment* and money.

Many great entrepreneurs play a game of trading off fulfillment quite often in the short-term so that they can achieve freedom in the long term. Like exercise, there is a certain delayed gratification to the entrepreneur game. True entrepreneurs love the game of business and often don't get excited by the actual business they are in. Instead, it's the *game* of business that drives them. Often, it's the multiples they can derive from the nature of the business. Insurance and call centers are examples of businesses that have great multiples but for many are not that stimulating in their own right.

The infopreneur who builds a practice and is a practitioner is playing a different game. The primary pursuit is not freedom; it is fulfillment. Using the concepts in this book, freedom is attainable — but whereas entrepreneurs are working to get themselves out of a business, practitioners are putting themselves into their practice. This idea is quite simplistic in nature, but fundamental to the thought leader's practice game plan.

These two games, the practice one and the business one, are not mutually exclusive concepts, but they are quite different games. They may look the same at first glance, but they definitely are not. There are principles that apply in one that do not apply in the other, and the outcomes of each are quite different.

PRACTICE	BUSINESS
Small team	Large team
Low start-up cost	High start-up cost
Based around expert	Based on systems
Has no value outside founder	Has value outside founder
Can't be sold	Can be sold
High profit margin	Low profit margin
Low overheads	High overheads
Can be cash-flow funded	Requires start-up funding
Highly agile & responsive to market	Less agile and less responsive

We are not making a case for one or the other — rather, a case to be clear which game you are playing. All three authors of this book have successfully run both practices and businesses. They are very different games with different rules and different strategies.

KNOW WHICH GAME YOU ARE PLAYING

If you play two games, you end up not playing either very well. Know the game you want to play and understand its rules. If you're playing the practice game, you need to understand how it differs from the common small business model. Then, if you get advice from a business expert, you know to take it with a grain of salt.

For example, media exposure is often great for a business. It drives awareness of who you are and what you do and can often lead to an increase in enquiries and, as a result, more business. In a practice, though, it's all about leveraging positioning. Some media channels, even if good press, will create the wrong kind of interest and perhaps tarnish your professional image. In a practice it's more about being professionally famous than it is about being known. This is a subtle example, but it helps to illustrate the different mindset needed to run a practice versus a business.

We come across many people running practices who are getting well-meaning but bad advice from people who know the game of business. Indeed, it's one of the big pitfalls of running a practice.

You have probably heard an accountant or business advisor say, "You have to stop trading your time for money". If you haven't heard that yet, you soon will. That's great advice for a business owner, and terrible advice for those of us running practices. We *are* in the game of trading our time for money — we just want to make sure the price of time is higher enough to keep us moving up the belts.

Likewise, you'll be told that you have to take your name off the door. Again, good advice for a business. Much harder to sell a business if it's based around the founder's name and brand. However, in a practice it *is* all about you, your brand, and your name. Your practice should literally be built around www.yourname.com.

How you conceptualize, plan, fund, market, sell, manage, document, grow and exit a practice is very different from how you do these things in a business.

In your practice, the primary focus is to *think*, *sell* and *deliver*. In the early stages you will probably be doing many other things too, from booking flights to sending invoices, but as the thought leader in your practice those are your main three functions. You need to do the thinking — create the intellectual property and turn it into activities that will make a contribution to people. It is then up to you to sell these services or products, to get in front of your target market, and to invite them to participate in one of your offerings. Finally, you deliver your services and/or products, whether it's a keynote speech or a coaching program, facilitating a process or developing workbooks.

WHEN TO RUN A PRACTICE AND A BUSINESS

There are people who successfully have both a business and a practice.

Richard Branson is the most obvious example. He runs a highly leveraged practice alongside his entrepreneurial ventures. He probably speaks around 50 times a year at, say, $75,000 an appearance; he sells his books through a major publisher; and he runs retreats to his island for entrepreneurs at around $25,000 a head for a weekend. Some rough numbers based on this create a picture of a practice turning over just shy of $9,000,000 a year — and doing so with less than 65 days a year of face time.

It's easy to review entrepreneurial models like Richard Branson to see the power that a star entrepreneur's personal brand can have on the business. People follow people, and a business led by a convincing and recognisable individual has a much greater chance of cutting through the clutter of modern marketing and reaching the hearts and minds of its customers.

Closer to home, Pete's accountant (and Thought Leaders graduate) Jason Cunningham uses his practice to feed his accounting business. He runs a full service accounting firm with over 50 staff, and at the time of writing is turning over just shy of $10M. He also has the Jason Cunningham Practice — Jase has written two books, has a weekly radio slot talking about money, is a regular on a couple of TV shows, speaks at conferences around Australia, and mentors about business and wealth strategies. His practice is at blue belt, but more importantly it is the primary source of new business for his accounting firm. Lots of people who hear Jase on the radio, see him speak, or read his books end up as clients of his firm, even if they never end up paying Jase personally for his advice.

If you want to run a thought leadership practice concurrently with a business, preparation is critical. When your business is established and systematized enough to run mostly without you, then you can take enough time away from the daily operations to focus on your practice.

2.

Cluster Strategy

The key to strategy is omission.

— Peter Drucker

A practice is like a patrol boat, while a business is more like a battleship. The battleship (business) needs to chart its course carefully and to be quite strategic about what it does. A practice (patrol boat) is more agile. It can explore tributaries and dash off on independent adventures. While not 100 per cent accurate, it might help to think of practices as being tactical and of businesses as being strategic. We realize that both models need both perspectives.

We believe that a practice should be built around a series of profitable projects, with each project being a profit center in its own right. Thought leaders should not be too concerned about some unified corporate strategy or about staying focused on their core business. Instead they know their overarching context and run their practice so that the projects they deploy are profitable and pleasurable. This agility is one of the key attractions to running a highly leveraged income-generating practice — it prevents us from becoming bored doing the same thing over and over! The cluster strategy is designed to help practices make money by organizing scarce resources and filtering attention into a series of specific focal points.

This rubs directly up against some entrenched ideas that are useful in building a business, but not as useful when running a thought leaders practice. It's brand *you*, to use a phrase coined by management author Tom Peters, that matters in a practice. Each year you can have different projects that you launch to new or existing markets that you have identified will benefit from your IP. Essentially, wherever there is a problem that your level of thinking can affect positively, go there. Don't do so in a scattered, haphazard way; rather, move from one concept to the next in a way that respects your highest context.

A profitable project is best defined in a thought leaders practice as some combination of message, market and method. We call any specific combination of these 3Ms a 'cluster'.

If you have ever had your eyes tested for spectacles or contact lenses, you will be familiar with the refraction tests using a phoropter. This is the test that your optometrist uses to determine your exact eyeglass prescription. During a refraction test, the optometrist places the phoropter in front of your eyes and shows you a series of lens choices. He or she will then ask you which of the two lenses in each choice looks clearer. Based on your answers, your optometrist will continue to fine-tune the lens power until the optimal eyeglass pre-scription is arrived at.

The three lenses we use to help thought leaders grow their prac-tices are your *message*, your *market* and your *method*. Like a refrac-tion test, there is a huge amount of variety in each category of lens.

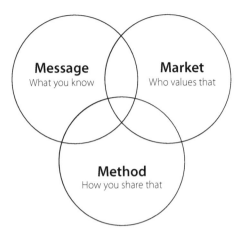

Each of these three areas is critical to building a successful practice. The following chapters describe this in further detail.

UNDERSTANDING CLUSTERS

These clusters are the secret to increasing the revenue in your practice, and moving up through the belts in the Thought Leaders Revenue Ladder. Everything we do is based on the cluster strategy.

For example, imagine your message is 'how to master your money and retire within 10 years'. Make sure that you have identified your market — for example: Generation Xers making an average income who are interested in wealth creation, investment and personal finance. You will also need to identify which mode of delivery you will use to achieve this. One delivery option with this example would be individual coaching, or you could deliver training workshops to groups of people on this message.

You can think of your clusters as spinning plates — like the ones on sticks at the circus. Your first cluster, your first $10,000 a month, is like your first plate. You make sure that's stable and spinning before you put up your second plate. You need to keep your first cluster ticking over at $10,000 a month while you are building up the second one — just don't let your first plate crash! A black-belt practice is typically made up of six clusters bringing in $10,000 a month each — six plates all spinning away.

Of course, in reality it never looks exactly like that. Some clusters will bring in $5,000 a month, others $20,000 a month. Different clusters will have different sales cycles. So even if a particular cluster brings in $120,000 a year, it's unlikely that it will be exactly $10,000 for each of the 12 months of the year. However, this is a great template to keep in mind, because while $60,000 a month might seem daunting and a million dollars a year might appear outright ridiculous, $10,000–$20,000 a month from one cluster is do-able. We just keep adding more of those. There are hardly any speakers, authors, trainers — any specialized individuals — making $720,000 a year from just one offering. The cluster strategy allows you to create this leverage.

The key strategy for building a black belt practice is to do so one step or one belt at a time. Our aim is to work up one mode at a time, gradually adding in others as we grow as a thought leader. If you have got to white belt as a trainer, then you should choose one of the other five modes — let's say mentor. Once you get to yellow belt with that, you'll pick a third modality to get to green belt.

In the Thought Leaders community there are a growing number of black belts who have got there using this model. The beauty of it is that the different modes build on each other. If you've written a book, it's much easier to get speaking gigs. Deliver a great keynote address, and people will want to buy your training program. Run a kick-ass training day, and you'll be in demand for your mentoring. And so on.

THREE YEARS TO BLACK BELT

We use a martial arts metaphor when we talk about the revenue in your thought leaders practice. The bottom level on the Thought Leaders Revenue Ladder is white belt, then yellow belt up to black belt. And like in a martial art you can then get a 2nd level black belt and a 3rd level black belt and so on.

BELT	INCOME	FOCUS
5th Dan	$1,200,000	Distribution
4th Dan	$1,080,000	Capacity
3rd Dan	$960,000	Productivity
2nd Dan	$840,000	Engagement
Black Belt	$720,000	Investment
Red Belt	$600,000	Leverage
Blue Belt	$480,000	Positioning
Green Belt	$360,000	Activity
Yellow Belt	$240,000	Value
White Belt	$120,000	Decision

Typically, the journey to black belt from zero is three years. Some thought leaders get there more quickly, and white belt to black belt has been done inside a year.

A successful cluster is one that brings in $10k a month. Each quarter we launch a new cluster — one every 90 days, making a total of four clusters launched a year. We think of each one as an experiment. Our hypothesis is that 'these people will pay this much money for this offering'. Then we go to market and test it.

We expect 50% to succeed and 50% to fail. We don't get attached to the results. They were only hypotheses, after all, and everything gives us useful feedback. Those that don't work we fail quickly, quietly, and cheaply. The ones that succeed we keep going, generating a belt ($10k a month).

At the end of three years we have launched twelve clusters, and half of them have succeeded. That means we have six clusters still going, generating $10k a month each, which is in total $60k a month, $720k a year… in other words, we're now at black belt.

GOING DEEPER INTO YOUR CLUSTERS

Here is the cluster model again, but with a few more points of detail at the intersections.

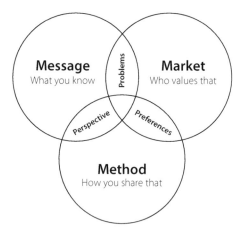

At the core of your *message* circle is the idea that you have a folder full of ideas (fleshed out in Intellectual Property Snapshots, which we'll come to). The folder is entitled 'Leadership' or 'Change', or some other abstract context word. All the individual ideas within it are then subsets of that big word. They have a relationship with that word at some level.

You want to have a step-by-step process that helps you build engagement with a person or group in your target market. It should walk through the problems that your market experiences daily, and link how your expertise might eliminate their problems.

The *method* circle is all about how you deliver your idea to the marketplace. The six most common delivery modes are speaker, author, trainer, mentor, facilitator and coach, and these are the key thinking we use to drive the method circle. Is there a particular mode most suited to your market? What modes have you already established yourself in? You select your modes based on the correct next mode in your practice rollout strategy.

INTERSECTIONS

First intersection — message and market

Where message and market intersect, you have a deep understanding of the *problems* your market experiences. You do this at three levels:

1. The problems someone is happy to express publicly.

2. The problems they express when admitting a deeper fear.

3. The problem as you, the expert, sees it.

The key is in making sure you move through these in this order, starting with what is comfortable for the receiver.

Critical to this intersection is a need to 'smarten your ideas down'. A room full of experts will indulge themselves in the jargon of their area of expertise. You should hear a room full of Thought Leaders Mentors discussing memes, the evolution of ideas, or the intricacies of a compelling IP Snapshot!

It's a natural and fabulous thing to be part of a conversation that is deeper because of a common knowledge platform. Nothing needs to be explained, and nuances are explored in a word and understood in a nanosecond. In our opinion, though, 'peers rarely pay' and as a result you need to be able to connect your expertise to the world of the novice.

We don't use the word 'novice' in a superior, dumb-it-down, patronizing way — this is why we say "smarten it down". We are all novices in something. This is about being commercially savvy enough to know how to take what you know and articulate it in a way that makes sense to others.

There are many references to the whole idea of problem solving scattered throughout this book, and you can also read more on this in *Thought Leaders*.

Second intersection — market and method

The second intersection is between your market and your method, and the word here is *preferences*. Preference works both ways; both for you and for the client or audience who receives what you offer.

Certain markets have a preference for certain communication methods.

When analyzing communication techniques, we find that they fall into three broad categories:

- **Tell moments**, where you deliver great ideas through stories and examples

- **Show moments**, where you educate your audience by sharing ideas and principles, and

- **Ask moments**, where you use the power of enquiry to lead people through your ideas.

Some audiences will want to be told, some will want to be shown, and some will want to be asked. It's easy to imagine, for example, that most leaders would prefer being asked a question around a topic, so that they can share their thoughts rather than simply being told what they need to do. Coaching them towards the solution may be more effective than telling them the answer. The market or audience for your message may have a communication preference, and you need to find it.

You, as the thought leader, may also have a preference for how you communicate to a certain market. If you truly love an industry and enjoy being involved day-to-day, you'll probably enjoy all the possible methods of delivery — whether speaking at conferences, training a room of people, facilitating discussion or coaching individuals. If, on the other hand, you've deliberately distanced yourself from the daily tasks of the industry in question, you might restrict yourself to speaking at conferences and mentoring executive leaders.

Third intersection — message and method

Where the message and method circles intersect, lies the idea of *perspective*. Every thought we sell has three dimensions: the content (concrete), the concept (specific), and the context (abstract). We build the architecture of an idea (these three levels) into a framework called an *IP Snapshot* so that we can in effect 'think once and use often'.

When you deliver these ideas to the market, sometimes you do so directly to individuals one-on-one, and sometimes to groups. Each of the six delivery modes we talk about in the Thought Leaders community falls into one of the three categories we discussed in *preference* — tell, show, and ask. These three categories align with the three dimensions of the idea captured in the IP snapshot:

- **Tell a story.** When keynote speaking, be sure to focus on content. For example, use stories that inspire, tell the relevance of your ideas, unpack a three-step process, share facts and statistics.

- **Show an idea.** When training or running a workshop, be sure to focus on the concept. For example, draw a model, make a point, present a case study of how the idea has worked already for someone else.

- **Ask a question.** When coaching people, be sure to focus on context. For example, ask questions that elicit content, get them to tell stories from their own experience, guide the conversation with your own model or metaphor.

Doing this ensures that you can use your great ideas again and again, in many different formats.

3.

The Ten Year Plan

*More people should learn to tell their dollars
where to go instead of asking them where they went.*

— ROGER BABSON

One of the criticisms of a practice compared to a business is that you can't sell a practice and retire off the money you get. It's a valid criticism, despite the fact that only a tiny percentage of businesses are successfully sold (but that's another story). Because your practice is based on you and your name, you can't count on selling it for a Lotto-like figure at the end of the journey. You possibly can't count on selling it at all. This means that when you are running your practice, you need to keep your expenses in both the practice and your lifestyle down, and to be investing significantly in appreciating assets outside of your practice.

Some of the highest-income earners in society are not wealthy. Sure, they have a high income — but no real net worth. It's easy to think that this is none of our business. Many people get touchy when you start to tell them what to do with their money. And to be absolutely clear: this book, and specifically this section, is not intended to be financial advice. We are not financial advisors.

Having a powerful relationship to money and personally achieving a level of financial mastery is critical to climbing the Thought Leaders Revenue Ladder. If you are powerful with money in your personal life and are successfully implementing your wealth plan to move towards financial independence, you will be more powerful financially in your practice. You will be able to price yourself appropriately. You won't feel desperate, greedy and ashamed … or boastful, showy and overly proud. In other words, you will be able to have clean conversations about money without the baggage that so many of us bring to that. Which is commercially smart.

Obviously, creating a wealth plan and establishing your financial independence is fabulous and desirable in itself. The extra bonus here is that doing so will make you more effective in your practice and help you move up the revenue ladder faster — which will result in you achieving your wealth plan sooner. It's a positive feedback loop that is all good. To build wealth and not just your income, you need to be effective at managing your money and growing your investments while you are building your practice.

FINANCIAL INDEPENDENCE

The real financial goal behind building your practice is to reach financial independence — to have enough money invested wisely in a diverse portfolio so that you can live off your investments for the rest of your life and never have to work again if you don't want to. It doesn't mean that you have to retire, or to retire permanently; it just means you have the freedom to. Being financially independent isn't about wearing socks up to your knees and taking up lawn bowls. Financial independence means that your passive income — the income from your investments — exceeds your living expenses.

It means that month-to-month, the money you get from your investments — the rent you receive from your investment properties or the dividends and interest you receive from your shares and investment funds — is more than you need to pay all your bills and expenses. Which, of course, means you can choose whether to work for money or not. Happy days if you get to black belt in three years and then run your practice at black belt and above for a decade and invest wisely along the way. You should have close to $5 million invested, and you can live off the interest and returns from that for the rest of your life.

There are three things, and three things only, that dictate how quickly you reach financial independence:

1. How much you earn

2. How much you spend

3. How well you invest

That's it. To reach financial independence sooner, you can earn more, spend less or invest better. Ideally, all three.

The first thing you need to do is to ensure that the income into your practice translates to take-home income for you. That means you want to keep the base costs of your practice low and ensure that most of the money flowing through your practice ends up in your pocket. You should be able to have a black-belt practice and beyond on a cost base of around $250,000. That means that if your practice is turning over $750,000, you should be taking home $500,000.

But earning that money on its own is only one-third of the equation. You also need to make sure you don't spend it all — that you create a substantial gap between what you earn and what you spend. And then you need to invest that gap money wisely. These last two pieces of the equation are just as important as the first. Much better to only make it to blue belt and still reach financial independence in 10 years, than get to black belt, spend everything and have nothing to show for it at the end.

There are two numbers to bear in mind here — $5 million and 10 years. Five million dollars is enough money for just about anybody to be comfortably financially independent. And 10 years is how long you have to run a black-belt practice for you to get there (you may well get there earlier, but 10 years is a good guideline of how long you can expect to maintain your practice for you to reach financial independence). Of course, you don't have to stop when you hit $5 million or after 10 years, but it's great to have that option available.

Let's look at what you need to do to get there.

Rock star your income, not your lifestyle

Thomas Stanley and William Danko wrote the bestselling book *The Millionaire Next Door: The Surprising Secrets of America's Wealthy*. The book is based on extensive historical research into the habits and characteristics of American millionaires. What they found surprised the authors. They expected millionaires to live in big houses in nice suburbs, drive top-of-the-range cars, and have expensive lifestyles. What they in fact found was that just as many of the millionaires lived 'next door' — they lived in normal houses in normal suburbs, drove normal cars, took normal holidays … they just happened to be wealthy.

Stanley and Danko reported that the top three characteristics of the millionaires were that they:

- Lived well below their means

- Prioritized financial independence over high social status

- Allocated time, energy, and money efficiently in ways conducive to building wealth

It turns out that high income wasn't one of the characteristics. The authors came across lots of millionaires on relatively low incomes, and lots of high-income earners with no assets to show for it. We propose that you want to emulate these millionaires — and be the millionaire next door. That means, first, living well below your means — creating a gap between what you earn and what you spend. This isn't what typically happens in our society — mostly our expenses rise to meet our income. As our income goes up, mysteriously so does our spending, and lo and behold there is still nothing left to invest.

In photography they talk about the rule of thirds — photos are typically more interesting if the subject is placed one-third of the way in from the edge rather than bang in the middle. The rule of thirds is also a good guideline for how the money that comes into your practice should be divided. One-third goes to the overheads, one-third goes to you to live on and one-third gets invested into your financial independence plan.

Second, you want to prioritize financial independence over high social status. In other words, prioritize wealth creation over looking good. It's tempting to go and buy the Porsche or the yacht or whatever your symbol of 'I've made it!' is. Don't. Once you've reached financial independence, if you still want it, then buy it. But in the meantime, prioritize financial independence.

We are actively creating a financial independence mindset within the Thought Leaders community. This means that when someone buys a brand-new sports car (that depreciated 20 per cent in the first 20 minutes they drove it), rather than being admiring we ask, 'Why did you do that?' We talk more about investments than about expensive toys. We want to be comfortable, have fun, live awesome lives, make great contributions — but not be excessive.

The final point we take from Stanley and Danko is to put the time and effort into building your wealth. Take responsibility for it; don't leave it to someone else.

The Thought Leaders methodology gives you the tools to rock star your income. If you can get to black belt or above in your practice on a cost base of $250,000 or below, that's at least half a million dollars that you are taking home. The trap here is the temptation that comes with that income to rock star your lifestyle.

As soon as you earn more money, the temptation is to spend more money, and still have nothing left over to invest. In real terms, people who do this are still poor — just poor, living in a bigger house in a 'nicer' suburb driving a better car.

There is nothing wrong with a bigger house, a nicer car, a better suburb, a holiday house, a yacht, first-class plane tickets, nice jewelry … whatever it is that lights your fire. And you can have all that. Just not yet. Hold out for 10 years, get $5 million invested, reach financial independence, and then go for your life. And by then, you'll find those things probably won't be that important.

Invest wisely in appreciating assets

The final piece of your wealth plan is to invest wisely. There are libraries of books written on the topic of investing, and obviously in this chapter we are only going to scratch the surface. We'll distinguish between active and passive investment strategies and give one example of a passive investment strategy. Of course, we don't know your individual financial circumstances and what's written here should not be construed as financial advice.

Active investment strategies are, as the name suggests, strategies that require your expertise, effort, engagement, and activity. If you are an expert in resource stocks, you study the companies and the markets in this sector and actively trade these stocks; that's an active strategy. Likewise, if you are into property investing, and buy, do up, and sell properties, that's another active strategy. If you have time, expertise and passion for a particular type of active investing, go for it. If not, you are probably better pursuing a more passive investment strategy and focusing your energy on making the money to invest from your practice.

A passive investment strategy is one that doesn't require a lot of time or expertise. For many Australians, your superannuation (or in the USA your 401(k)) is probably invested in a managed fund. For most people this is a common form of passive investing. Investing in a low-cost index fund (which Warren Buffet recommends for unsophisticated investors) is also a common passive investment strategy. Other passive investments can involve property investment without the 'fixing up' strategy.

We don't want to tell you which one to do — the important thing is to pick one that works for you and get the professional advice that assists you in your decision. Also, remember to pick a financial advisor who has made their money from the successful implementation of their strategies. We know of too many financial planners who made their money from recommending investments that they had never owned and that they wouldn't invest in personally. If you are looking for a financial advisor, ask them about their investment portfolio, how they made their money, and what strategies they used. If they won't answer these questions you might want to find someone who can.

Your wealth plan

The plan is to use your practice to create financial independence — at least $5 million invested wisely in appreciating assets that you can live off for the rest of your life if you choose to. The aim is to get there in 10 years or less.

To do this, implement the strategies found within this book to increase the income from your practice to $720,000 a year or more within three years, and then maintain it at that level. Make sure that when you do that you keep the overheads in your practice low — one-third or less is a good guideline — so that your take-home pay is good.

Then keep your spending under control so that you are investing a good chunk of your 'take-home' cash — ideally more than half. Finally, invest that amount wisely so that it grows to your $5 million and beyond as quickly and securely as possible.

Your Message

4.

The Power of Expertise

If you find from your own experience
that something is a fact and it contradicts
what some authority has written down,
then you must abandon the authority and
base your reasoning on your own findings.

— Leonardo da Vinci

The information age has radically changed the way expertise is valued and accessed. Anyone can use Google and Wikipedia to get a quick overview of almost any subject. It used to be that expertise was a prized possession, something that was hard to get access to and something we had to pay a premium for if we could find it. Of course, that is no longer the case. Even medical specialists face informed patients who are motivated and well-read on alternative cures and trial medicines.

Of course, a little knowledge on a lot of topics can be dangerous. There is still a role for subject-matter experts. Now, however, it's not enough to know what you know. You have to be able to share what you know in way that engages people. The days of the aloof academic are numbered. Experts must evolve into thought leaders!

Subject-matter experts are those people with knowledge about how to do things better. They have something to offer an industry or a sector. They make a difference as what they know has a direct impact on how others do things in a better way. They are thought leaders. They are innovators and original thinkers.

Often they don't realize that they are, and even if they do, they don't always have the skills to communicate those ideas in a way that others understand. In a recent study by Rainmaker, the online platform for sales and marketing professionals, speaking at conferences and tradeshows and producing white papers were ranked as some of the best ways of selling any product or service. People trust informed people, and expertise and authority are true business currencies.

CREATE ONCE — USE OFTEN

In business leverage occurs when you build once then you can sell often. At Thought Leaders we are focused on thinking once and delivering often — which reduces the need to reinvent over and over.

The goal is to build your intellectual property in a way that is able to be delivered in multiple ways. This allows you to leverage your ideas even further. Also it is important to ensure that whatever your intellectual property is, it can be packaged and delivered into any one of the six core delivery modes available to you. You want to create something that you can write a book on, speak at a conference on and deliver a one on one mentoring session on—all around a similar message. Once you have clarified your domain of expertise, the aim is to deliver it in numerous ways to numerous audiences.

The thing that differentiates a thought leaders approach from others is the demand it places on you to come up with great ideas first. Its quality of idea before size of market. It's absolutely not about internet marketing with 'keyword searches' or 'click-generated revenue'. It's about taking the ideas in your head and making the most

44

of them commercially. It's not about finding a gap in the market and exploiting it. It's for thinkers. By building a bank of ideas you get to generate more great ideas and sell them to different markets in a host of different ways. You may be able to get rich making money in your pajamas behind a computer screen, but really, is that any way to live?

This is the beauty of clusters. They allow you to take the same message and deploy it into different markets. As previously mentioned, we focus on launching a new cluster every 90 days. This could involve you either taking a message and targeting a new market, or developing a new message and targeting another market. The important point is to have your ideas created and to be able to leverage them numerous times.

CREATE A FOLDER OF IDEAS

To assist you in capturing and organizing your thoughts we recommend that you create a number of folders of intellectual property that capture ideas that you can use. This is more than a way to keep a number of ideas together, it will allow you to further develop and commercialize these ideas.

Most people will have a number of topics that they want to create or to clarify their expertise in. For one person they may want to be viewed as an expert in innovation. Another person may want to be known for inspiration and storytelling. Regardless of what your expertise is, we recommend that you start to capture a number of thoughts, articles and book summaries on these topics and put these in individual folders to help provide you with more background and to create a working library that you can continue referring back to.

One method that you can use to capture the areas that you want to develop your IP around can be by writing the individual topics that you are interested in on a separate sticky note for each idea. We find that five to seven individual sticky notes of ideas or topics that you want to explore are a good place to start. Place these sticky notes with these words on a wall and see if you can identify any correlation between the topics. It may be that there is an order or hierarchy to them or it may be that each of these individual topics is a subset of another topic. Often these initial sticky notes become your domains of expertise and the labels on your folders.

YOUR DECK OF 52

Ideally each IP folder you create would have at least 52 distinct ideas that are fully formed and fully thought out around a specific topic that you want to become an expert in. Although this sounds simple, it is no quick and easy task. The quality of the thinking needs to meet the criteria we described earlier and ensure full spectrum thinking.

Because of this rigor and depth of thinking, we call this a 'Commercial PhD.' This can earn you the right to identify yourself as an expert because of the quality of thought that is relevant, thorough, elegant and unique. Also the conviction that is gained from creating this many ideas can cement your expertise at an even deeper level. The tool we use to capture these ideas is the Intellectual Property Snapshot — more on that soon.

If you use a deck of 52 playing cards as an analogy you can start to understand that each folder of ideas will have a range of ideas that will have different values. Some ideas that you capture will be incredible and when others see them they are inspired — these would be considered your Ace, King or Queen cards. As you are exploring your ideas you will also have a number of ideas that are not as fabulous. They may either be not as clear and not as valuable, or they may simply be good ideas that support your great ideas. At this stage it is important to go for quantity to ensure that you identify as many thoughts around a topic as possible — and you will then use the IP Snapshot process to add quality to the idea.

POSITIONING IN MULTIPLE DOMAINS

As you create a range of ideas that are organized in folders with at least 52 great concepts captured, you will begin to grow your expertise. Remember that the goal is to not stick to only one domain of expertise. We all know of someone who tells a great story from the past, and unfortunately does not have any other new ideas or stories in their repertoire. So every time you bump into this person they continue to share the same story that they have been talking about for the past 20 years. In today's world this is a recipe for disaster. Do not get stuck here!

Your goal is to create three to seven domains of expertise. Over time you will develop a strategy to position yourself in different markets using different delivery modes to share this expertise. However, at the beginning you will need to have a strategy that captures your brilliant ideas so that you can share them with others.

WHAT YOU KNOW MATTERS

We suggest that thought leaders dedicate themselves to crafting a compelling message, shaping their ideas so that people see the quality of thought behind their work. Too many people focus on method or market first. When we create our clusters (our combination of message, market and method) we say start with your message. Coming from message gives you the best chance to build your thought leadership around true expertise. If you consider your market first you are more prone to extending yourself into domains you know little about just because of a perceived market opportunity. This then increases the risk of plagiarizing others' work (uncool), or simply not 'connecting' enough in the marketplace because your ideas don't extend the body of work that already exists on the subject.

Time taken to clarify and identify what you know is never time wasted. The challenge is to ensure that you have a process that captures your ideas or intellectual property in a way the can be leveraged commercially — so people will pay you to learn more about it. We'll look at how to do that in the next chapter.

As a thought leader you will want to craft messages that work towards four outcomes:

- **Relevant**: It meets a need and solves a problem.

- **Thorough**: It has depth of meaning that stands on its own.

- **Elegant**: It is captured in a way that is simple and clean.

- **Unique**: It adds insights or value in new ways.

As you move your ideas along these four stages the ideas become more valuable. Literally, the amount you can charge for them increases. We have found this to be true for the thousands of people who have followed the process. But you need to develop your ideas as continual works in progress.

VALUE OF IDEA		EXAMPLE FEE
4	Unique	$10,000
3	Elegant	$7,500
2	Thorough	$5,000
1	Relevant	$2,500

Thought leadership becomes more commercially valuable the more unique characteristics it has. If it doesn't have a unique perspective or new insight, then it's probably thought repetition. The trick is discovering what your unique perspective is and then using that to inform your great ideas.

This is akin to branding in business. The essence of who you are needs to shine in your thought leadership. If you have a contrary nature, then you need to learn how to position your ideas so that they are congruent with this attitude. It's a form of branding your thoughts and you need to create an identify that supports your profitable practice and influences your ideas.

FULL-SPECTRUM IDEAS

When you first think of any idea it's typically incomplete. It's like looking at an object from one point of view and determining that the shape of the object is a circle, it's only when you travel around the object and get some perspective that you see it's actually a sphere. It's the same thing with your ideas — you need to travel around them and get some perspective. This makes your thinking more robust and your ideas able to be leveraged.

It's commercially smart as a thought leader to structure your messages so that they appeal to many different thinking styles and are applicable in many different situations. Your ideas should dance across the full spectrum of left-brain logic through to right-brain creativity, and then from concrete, specific examples up to high-order contextual ideas.

This process of full spectrum thinking is key to the thought leaders practice model. You want to develop your ideas so that they are mode agnostic. Don't write a speech, or plan a coaching session, as a way of creating IP. Think before you speak, coach, or mentor. Thought leaders think through ideas all the time, realizing that this thinking time is 'intellectual property development.' It's the capital and equity in the thought leaders practice game. If a business has $520,000 in equity or capital to keep it afloat a practice needs 52 well thought out ideas to be in the same position. Ideas float practices.

SPECTRUM MODEL

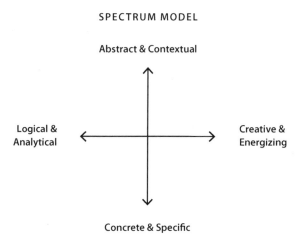

Abstract & Contextual

Logical & Analytical   Creative & Energizing

Concrete & Specific

As expressed in the Spectrum Model, you can see that every idea exists at various levels of abstraction (the vertical axis). At one end of the scale, you have very concrete expressions of an idea; at the other end, there are very abstract expressions of it. This is an important part of unlocking expertise.

The ideas also exist at various levels of logic and creativity (the horizontal axis). Like the hemispheres of the brain, we need to mix logic and emotion. We need to have our ideas available so they appeal to both logos and pathos.

When people sit down to craft their message it can be a battle between putting in too much information, which results in the essence of the idea being lost, or transmitting so simple a message that it is not seen as practical or relevant by those listening to it.

Thought leaders are positioned as experts because of their ability to capture their expertise and share it with others. They do not just 'do this.' Often what appears as a simple message has actually been a well-planned and crafted idea that captures the intellect in a unique way.

You need to create full-spectrum ideas.

TAKING IT TO THE NEXT LEVEL

To be considered an expert you need to be able to capture the idea that is currently in your head in a way that others can easily understand. Then if you do this enough times and create something new in the world you will become known for knowing something.

Craft your ideas into a format that achieves three outcomes:

- **Clarity**: It is a clear message that is accessible to most people most of the time.

- **Flexibility**: It can be used repeatedly in different formats.

- **Integrity**: It is received by others in a way that retains the original meaning.

And that's what the Intellectual Property Snapshot does. It creates snapshots to help others quickly present an overview of key ideas. It lets you as the thought leader unpack your IP rapidly, consider the ideas across the full spectrum, and shuffle them around so they can use the same idea in lots of different ways. We think it's the big idea that makes the thought leaders practice game fly.

ANATOMY OF AN IDEA

There is a certain architectural element to thinking before you speak, and this structure or design can help you engage more people more of the time as a thought leader. It's about seeing an idea in all its layers simultaneously.

For ease of understanding, let's limit the layers of an idea to three:

- The stuff you say that is specific (content)

- The point you are making (concept)

- The big picture theme that the idea is a part of (context)

ANATOMY OF AN IDEA

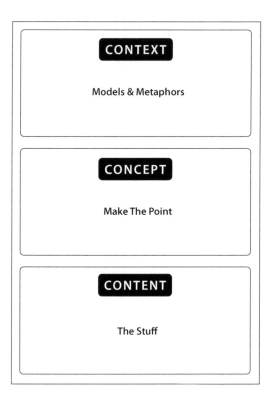

Each idea or point should be able to be captured on a single sheet of paper. It creates a depth around your ideas and forces you to create messages with substance and balance. There are three clear sections to an idea: the first is the middle third, or the concept section; the second is the content section at the bottom; and the last is the context section at the top.

5.

Intellectual Property Snapshots

A mind, once stretched by a new idea,
never regains its original dimensions.

— OLIVER WENDELL HOLMES

If you're to be commercially successful as a thought leader, the first thing you have to do is have some thoughts. If you're to do this profitably, it makes sense to have a system of capturing and developing your ideas. Intellectual Property Snapshots are the primary tool that we teach to do this. This process allows you to take a fragment of an idea and develop it to a level that reaches a higher level of thinking. It is at the core of what we believe in and is used to position you as the expert.

As discussed we encourage people to create multiple sets (folders) of IP Snapshots around various domains of expertise. You might have a folder full of ideas on leadership, another with ideas on service, and yet another with ideas on authenticity.

The IP Snapshot process lets you capture ideas without worrying too much about the specific applications of those ideas. That comes later. If you have your ideas worked out well, you'll be able to repurpose what you know for a variety of different markets. If your ideas are only captured form-specific to a particular industry (e.g. finance) or category of applications (e.g. marriage counseling), you lose the power of easily leveraging the same core idea into different commercial advice applications.

You may have heard IP Snapshots referred to as 'Pink Sheets' within the Thought Leaders community. When Matt first created and printed the IP Snapshot he didn't realize the printer was full of pink paper (what the pink paper was doing in the printer has been lost in the annals of history). The term pink sheet was coined, and, along with the color, it's stuck.

FIVE COMPONENTS OF AN IP SNAPSHOT

The IP Snapshot builds on the *Anatomy of an Idea,* and provides the necessary layers and structure to allow you to capture your thoughts at a much deeper level. There are five components that make up an IP Snapshot and here below we share the 5 most obvious tools for each component:

1. Model (for logical context)

2. Metaphor (for creative content)

3. Declarative Point (for central concept)

4. Case Study (for logical content)

5. Story (for creative content)

5 COMPONENTS OF IP SNAPSHOT

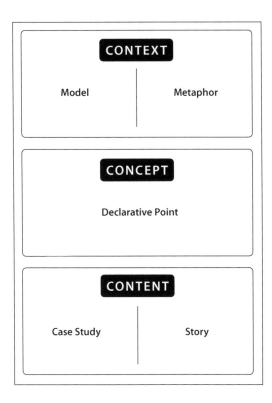

CREATING CONTEXT: MODELS & METAPHORS

One way to create *context* is to create a visual model of your ideas. Creating context above every point you wish to make is a master thought leaders tool. This is the ideas context. It is the 'big picture' representation of your idea. Often this is a diagram, model, metaphor, an allegory or some applicable quotes.

This context then provides a broad framework to give people a map to a message or line of thought. People are often engaged as they get the purpose of the detail, and if they get lost, they can refer to your initial map. You are setting out the architecture of the idea, the framework that all the detail will be built around.

Models (left brain)

A model is geometric in nature and consists of squares, lines, circles, triangles, pentagons and graphs, as well as every variation and combination of these elements (see opposite page).

At its simplest expression, a model is a visual representation of your key idea. The word above each model is simply a starting point for consideration, to assist you in quickly identifying which dynamics can be described by which model.

Whether it's a quadrant, some concentric circles, a pyramid or even a simple triangle, a model helps you make more than one point. It helps define the conversational boundaries of any discussion.

Some great models are:

- Abraham Maslow's *Hierarchy of Needs*

- Stephen Covey's *First Things First*

- Robert Kiyosaki's *Cash Flow Quadrant*

Become a model kleptomaniac. Capture and clipboard every model you see. Study the anatomy of models, tracking their structure, their design and their intent.

Metaphors (right brain)

Metaphors are object- and activity-based, and can be sourced from real life and everyday examples. When using a metaphor, you target the right hemisphere of people's brains. This allows you to ensure

MODEL MENU

relationships
(simple)

hierarchy

unity

progress

returns

evolution

choices

curriculum

focus

relationships
(distinctions)

timelines

relationships
(complex)

that your ideas are developed with full spectrum thinking that has depth.

Here are some starting ideas for finding an appropriate metaphor:

- **Instruments** (measuring and feedback):
  compass, clock, thermometer, map

- **Transport** (movement and effort):
  boat, car, train, plane, rocket

- **Creating** (art and combining): painting, building, sculpting

- **Professions** (quality and process): medicine, law, accounting

- **Trade**: plumber, carpenter

- **Nature** (growth and order): spider's web, pool of water,
  bamboo, trees

- **Universe** (scale and relationships): stars, orbit, gravity

- **Sport** (roles and responsibilities): positions
  for players, game comparison

- **Interests**: make a list of your hobbies and interests

Models and metaphors are in no way the only tools of context, but they are a great start. You may also want to consider icons, fables, idea hierarchies and stacked metaphors.

CREATING CONCEPT: MAKING THE POINT

If the context is the big picture around an idea, the *concept* is where you give these ideas specific meaning. The concepts are the point around which all your models, metaphors, case studies and stories pivot.

Be clear on the point of your idea — why is this important for others to know. You should be able to summarize your idea in one or two simple sentences that explain the whole point. From this singular idea you then create several different ways of delivering it.

There are also two parts to making a point. The first is a specific declarative statement. It can be something you believe to be true or something that needs to be realized by others. When trying to identify a specific point that you are trying to capture, it can be useful to think of a bumper sticker or a title of a book. The second part of making a point is a one-sentence explanation of what the declarative statement means. This provides a succinct layer to provide the point you are trying to make.

When the idea is captured it then helps to run it through several other palette layers. How might it be said simply, or inspiringly, or practically, or wisely? These extra linguistic palettes are like clarity filters forcing you to say the same thing lots of different ways. You have to be really clear about what your idea is to achieve this. Use these six linguistic palettes as a checklist for the different ways of expressing your ideas. This process, like each stage in the IP Snapshot, will shape your thinking.

1. Formal

2. Casual

3. Simple

4. Inspiring

5. Practical

6. Sagacious

CREATING CONTENT: THE 'STUFF'

The *content* is the detailed and practical section of the IP Snapshot and is often found in case studies and stories. Gather examples, facts, stories and other detail elements to support or explain your point. Like the big idea, you need to balance this to cover the whole brain.

Case studies (left brain)

Case studies are logical stories that fulfill the left hemisphere of the brain. They contain facts and figures that provide an analytical perspective with data and information. The best case studies have a real world vibe to them that can be viewed as factual story telling. They also have a structure that generally covers three areas: *incident*, *point* and *benefit*. The incident is what actually happened. It can be captured a number of ways from describing what happened to what this really means to how you can use this information. One method that can be used is sharing some statistics around a particular issue (incident), describing what is actually causing these statistics (point), and then how this information can help them (benefit).

Some case study strategies include:

- Set the scene — when delivering the case study, ensure that you take the time to explain why this case study matters to the audience.

- Ensure relevance — make sure that the case study you are sharing will resonate with your audience. The most powerful case studies are those which people can relate to on a personal level.

- Integrate statistics — the logical brain quickly grasps statistics as they are quantifiable and easy to understand. You can add more depth by stacking statistics back to back, which often demonstrates a deeper level of understanding or expertise in a topic.

Other left brain content tools that you can use to share detail include:

- A step by step process

- A set of statistics that create meaning

- A graph or table

- An infographic

- A book reference that supports the idea

You are making your point with real concrete examples.

Stories (right brain)

Stories are the vignettes that carry a message which connects with and inspires others. Everyone can remember stories from their childhood. Most stories describe a tale that had a range of ups and downs, and generally resulted in people living happily ever after. The powerful stories also had a point or a moral to the story that was memorable over time. Can you remember the story about the *Boy that cried wolf*?

Some thoughts around stories:

- People or organizations that people admire can provide great inspirational stories. With admiration, many people are often more open minded, and so able to listen and learn.

- When sharing a story ensure that you bring it to life, become the characters, speak as they speak, and ensure that you relive the story — not just recite it!

- Stories can be powerful when they include a mix of personal, topical and historical. Just be careful about sharing stories about yourself that make you the hero — many audiences can be turned off by this approach. If telling a personal story, it is better to share one that is self-deprecating and humorous.

Other right brain detail tools that you can use include:

- Photos of actual places and people

- Biographical pieces around a relevant quote

- Movie extracts, scripts that make the point

- Songs or poems played, recited shared

- Show a video that supports the point

You are bringing the idea alive in the mind of your audience or client.

To assist you in seeing an IP Snapshot (Pink Sheet) in action we have drafted a sample one on productivity (see opposite page). Take a few minutes to read through it. You should be able to see how the point is made, how models and metaphors are used to visualize the context, and how detailed facts further support the content.

In this example the model is a 2x2 quadrant model. The metaphor is adjustable high tech binoculars.

The concept is expressed in two different palettes, both formal and casual. The formal is the 'productive adaptation' piece and the casual is the 'work smarter not harder' statement.

The left brain content tool is the 5 steps in each of the lower quadrants. Another is a walkthrough of all the books and thinkers so far on personal effectiveness.

The right brain content tools are the exercise around how you read a book and a story around how Matt writes books.

SAMPLE IP SNAPSHOT

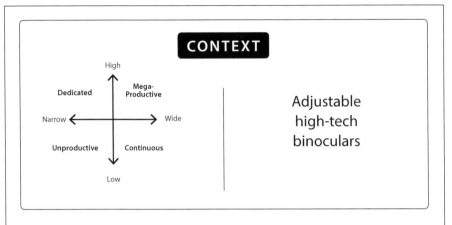

CONTEXT

High

Dedicated | Mega-Productive

Narrow ← → Wide

Unproductive | Continuous

Low

Adjustable high-tech binoculars

CONCEPT

Productive adaptation!
Know whether wide or narrow focus is your preference and develop productivity habits that complement and extend your work practices.

Work smarter not harder!
Get better at knowing how to support your natural way of working.

CONTENT

Role distinctions
Chunk time
Distraction management
Contextual clarity
Planned spontaneity

Discipline pleasure
Get out more
Learn something new
Be accountable to someone
Turn off better

Dedicated capturing tools
Objective clarity
Completion focus
Productivity blitzes
Static distraction

How do you read a book, exercise and split the room?

Evolution of personal effectiveness

My book writing process

UNPACKING AN IP SNAPSHOT

When unpacking your IP Snapshot to an audience, we encourage you to adapt your delivery depending upon your experience and that of your audience. There isn't a set way that is the most effective in sharing your idea. We have found, however, that there is a strategy to unpacking your IP Snapshots to an audience — especially one that is skeptical. This can be achieved by presenting your ideas from left to right — starting by presenting with a logical emphasis first, and an emotional emphasis second.

You start by sharing your model (position 1) to show the logical framework for people to follow. You next share a metaphor (position 2) that engages the audience with a more abstract and creative perspective. This is followed by the point that you are trying to make (position 3). This is then further enhanced with a case study that provides the practical and analytical detail (position 4). You can then transition from here to telling a story (position 5) to demonstrate what this really means and to engage the audience at a more emotional or personal level.

Again, there is no set formula. We have included this strategy to assist those who are just getting started or have been struggling with unpacking their IP Snapshot.

We do recommend that you start by delivering at a contextual level before going into the detail of what you are trying to communicate. This is often a rookie mistake that is made when people try to share everything they know without giving people a visual map to follow (model) or a specific context for them to be thinking around (metaphor). Context is quick to share. When delivering the specific details or content, take some more time to get through it.

6.

Capture Your Genius

No army can withstand the strength of
an idea whose time has come.

— VICTOR HUGO

So how do you start to create your own ideas and capture them into your IP Snapshots? There are a range of different strategies that people use. We have found that there are three common methods that can be particularly useful.

METHOD 1: IDENTIFY WHAT YOU KNOW ALREADY

Many thought leaders have hundreds if not thousands of ideas bouncing around in their head. Capture these ideas. You can use the sticky note method described earlier. Generate at least 5-7 things that you know to be true about the topic and place these on a wall. Move them around and look for any correlation that you can find between the ideas that can assist you in generating your idea. Try to identify the big word that is at the essence of the point that you are trying to make.

From here you can start creating models that show the relationship between a number of the concepts that you are thinking around. You can then then look at possible metaphors and case studies and stories to complete your pink sheet. Remember, it can take time for your ideas to land, so be patient and allow the process to occur!

METHOD 2: USE QUOTES FOR INSPIRATION

Another method that you can use is to identify a quote that you find inspirational or sums up the point that you want to explore and develop ideas around. When you are creating your IP Snapshots and layering your content you can refer back to this original thinker and show how you are expanding on their initial thought.

You can Google these quotes or principles to identify what others have said about this topic. You then start expanding on this simple thought with your additional ideas and thoughts. Feel free to use the post-it-note method we described earlier to help you capture this.

METHOD 3: CONDUCT A LITERATURE REVIEW OF BEST SELLERS

Books that are best sellers have captured an idea in a way that others understand, admire and support. These best-selling books can also be used as a way to generate your ideas. This is not dissimilar to someone writing a thesis for their master's degree when they conduct a review of the literature to identify and build upon the ideas that others have already published.

Someone that is an expert needs to have background knowledge and understanding of how others view the same particular idea. So your review of best sellers needs to be across three categories: *current*, *contemporary* and *classic*.

Current

These are the books that are the most popular at the given moment. They tend to be the leading edge or trends that people are looking for or listening to. It is important to be across these because others will be reading and talking about them due to their being recent and often representing current positioning across the marketplace. Bookstores and newspapers actively promote the current best sellers.

Contemporary

These best sellers are those that are enduring over time. They may not be current and they are not quite the classics, however they have captured the essence of an idea that others remember and admire. They often were the best sellers or trendsetters in the past that people now want to learn more about.

Classic

Classics are the cornerstone books that often initiated a particular line of thinking. They encapsulated an idea that was so totally new from the past that they became classics. Some of the content may not be relevant in the current time, however the essence of the ideas often provide value.

When reading these best sellers read at a higher level of understanding. A basic reader will read a book and think: '*That is interesting*.' A teacher will read a book and start thinking: '*How can I teach that?*' A thought leader will read a book, highlight the relevant points, and start asking themselves: '*What do I think about this?*'

IDEAS COME FROM CONTRIBUTION AND CONTRADICTION

We use a simple technique when rethinking established ideas. As you come across an idea in a book or blog, ask yourself not: '*What are they saying?*' but rather: '*What do I think about that?*' Often original thinking will come from a 'yes AND' or a 'yes BUT' place.

One method to use is to have two pads of paper available when you read a book. At the top of one pad label it: 'And,' and at the top of the other label it: 'But.'

As you read through the books, capture your thoughts on these pads of paper and capture them on one or the other. If it is something you agree with and want to expand on, then you capture it in the 'And' pad. If there is something that you disagree with or want to contradict, write it on the 'But' pad.

It is in the contributions and contradictions to existing ideas that you can add your piece to an existing thought. Thought leaders don't just read or highlight the books they read, they add to them.

You can take these ideas — which are now your ideas — and capture them as the key points that you want to expand on. Once again you can use the IP Snapshot to start filling in your structure around these ideas.

YOUR IP AND OTHERS' IP

Thought leaders need to come up with original ideas. Their intellectual property needs to bring new thinking to a field of expertise. But how do you know when an idea is yours and when it is not?

> *If I have seen further than others, it's because*
> *I have stood on the shoulders of giants.*
>
> — Isaac Newton

'The shoulders of giants' has become a metaphor for developing intellectual pursuits by understanding the works of past notable thinkers. Ironically, Isaac Newton's aphorism, much used as a bumper sticker for expertise, humility and plagiarism, was based on an utterance of Bernardus Carnotensis (Bernard of Chartres), a twelfth-century French philosopher, who in AD 1124 said (in Latin): *Nanos gigantium humeris insidentes.* Translation: 'Dwarfs standing on the shoulders of giants.'

So when is it not your idea?

When are you a 'thought repeater'?

There is a reason that the academic community has been obsessed with original thinking and plagiarism. An anti-plagiarism culture means great thinkers are more likely to share if their ideas are attributed. Yes, this is good for the ego of the original thinker and source. But it is more than that. It's also good for the person who acknowledges the source. It creates a base for them to stand on and from which to create their own original ideas. It is as if plagiarism and the passing off of ideas as your own fills your head with a kind of anti-creative dust. If you want to advance your thinking, become obsessed with attribution.

In the Thought Leaders community, whenever we want to share a piece of IP developed by one of our colleagues, we introduce it with something along the lines of the following attribution script.

My Friend [insert thought leader's name] is an expert on [insert thought leader's positioning message]. He created a brilliant framework called [insert the name of IP piece as expressed by the source]. You can learn more about it from [insert website or book title, etc]. I'd love to share it with you today.

Then we share the IP. This is commercially smart and energetically right. Start doing this with every idea any thought leader shares with you and watch:

- Your status and credibility go up in the room

- Your own creativity and original thinking go up a notch

- Great thinkers begin to share your ideas in exchange.

In the information economy era we need to upgrade the plagiarism mindset. We need to move from plagiarism to attribution. It is less about the fear of thievery and more about the power of attribution. In fact, the creative commons movement has even created an alternative to the established practice of copyright. They have coined the term 'copyleft', which is represented with an inverted copyright symbol. Copyleft basically means that anyone is free to copy and even to circulate the material on the understanding and commitment that they will acknowledge where the material or writing was developed. It means naming the original source and attributing the idea (or IP) to its creator.

Matt Church is a master of this. When he speaks he will invariably name three experts in the room and their thinking and three amazing books or points of reference. This only serves to strengthen and place his ideas as original. This also serves to help him build advocacy around his ideas. He honors the source as often as possible and in turn is honored for his.

In fact, attribution encourages the pooling and sharing of IP in a way that turns potential plagiarism into positive promotion. In effect, the problem of plagiarism becomes an instrument for building advocacy.

Be a *thought promoter*, not a *thought stealer*!

A SEVEN-STEP PROCESS FOR BUILDING YOUR IDEAS

1. Create a list

Write a numbered list of all the things you know, talk on, or may like to share with others. If they are across several fields of expertise, build a list for each field of expertise. Think of these ideas as simple bumper stickers that concisely capture the essence of your idea.

2. Identify idea clusters

Know the difference between an idea and a cluster of ideas. An idea has only a few key points associated with it. If you brainstormed all the points around your idea and came up with more than three points, it is probably a few ideas clustered together. Break the cluster down or chunk it up until you have a clear idea that has, for example, three central points.

3. Have a point

Be clear on the point of your idea. We call this the concept. You should be able to summarize your idea as one or two simple sentences that explain the whole point. From this single idea, you then create several different ways of saying it.

4. Make it a big idea

Try to represent the idea broadly so it is non-specific and can be related to by as many people as possible. We call this the ideas context. It is the 'big picture' representation of your idea. Often this is a diagram, model, metaphor, an allegory or some applicable quotes.

5. Support your point

Gather examples, facts, stories, case studies and other detail elements to support or explain your point. We call this content. As in the case of the big idea, you need to balance this to cover the whole brain.

6. Create a folder system

Document the idea in a searchable, retrievable system. At Thought Leaders, we call this our *Folder* system that contains all of your great ideas — including the minimum of 52 individual thoughts that will create you.

7. Customize content, not context

Finally, constantly review your Folders, particularly in the content area. It is the content that changes most, not the concept or the context. If you clearly think out concepts and can represent them in any context, all you need to worry about is what content you will use to create a connection with your audience. Getting good at this allows you to repeat key ideas over and over, with people hearing them again as if for the first time.

An idea is created, not innate. To have an idea is to create a document that can be better read than said. That's like saying you write a performance, but of course, you don't. You write a song and then you create a performance.

Your Market

7.

Clicking with Value

If you work just for money, you'll never make it.
But if you love what you're doing, and always
put the customer first, success will be yours.

— RAY KROC

Once you have your IP Snapshots and folders full of ideas, you need to assess who will care about them enough to pay money for them. Whose problems do your ideas solve? Until you have spent the time thinking through your message, you have no idea who will really benefit from it. Classic entrepreneurism starts with the market opportunity; thought leadership requires an element of 'you' first. So the second perspective to create your clusters from is the *market for your message*. You gain experience and subject-matter expertise before you explore who will benefit from them.

NICHE NUANCES

When marketing your practice, you need to resist opportunistic thinking. This is quite challenging and again flies in the face of traditional business advice. Typically, people start businesses by spotting a gap in the marketplace and creating a solution for that. It's an outside-in approach. Iconic marketing gurus such as Jay Abrahams will advise that market comes first: start by identifying a hungry market and then work out how to fill the need. It's great advice for a business — but not the best approach for a practitioner.

Rather than looking for a gap in the marketplace that you can then craft a value proposition for, you should begin by exploring what you know and what you care about. You then want to ask yourself how you feel about serving your target market. Put simply, do you think that if you had to spend time away from your family or loved ones that you would be happy to spend that time on your target market?

Niche marketing is an awesome way to get any business started, and we love specialization. However, whilst a business typically has one or two niche specialty markets, a practice often has many! (We realize that many specializations is an apparent oxymoron.)

For a practice to work profitably, you often need to have multiple niches. That means you will focus on several markets at the same time. You just don't communicate with them all in the one marketing conversation. Both specialization and diversity make sense; it's simply that they contradict when viewed at the same time. Specialize in a specific market but diversify your delivery methods. Or specialize in a particular message and diversify your markets.

As you can see in the diagram on the opposite page, it's all about finding your angle. As a subject-matter expert, you have a message that is the primary driver for how you commercialize your ideas. The focus on market is then from a message-out focus, not a market-in approach. Rather than asking '*What does a specific market need?*' you ask, '*How does what I know serve a specific market?*'

Subject-matter experts tend to develop their expertise within a certain market segment. This does not mean that they should limit that expertise to that market only. When you separate the technical specific content of your expertise and begin to see it as transferable principles and concepts, you can leverage what you know into different markets.

FIND YOUR ANGLE MODEL

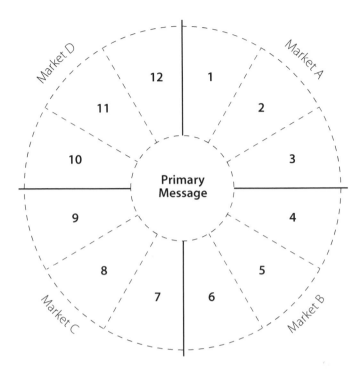

There are two things to consider with this:

1. For many, the first cross-over market requires a certain leap of faith. Typically people have spent so long in one particular market that they are squarely in the centre of their comfort zone. Our advice: take the leap!

2. Once you have a primary master message, you then leverage into select markets. We show four in the diagram but you could cut each quarter once or twice more. This would create up to 12 different markets for your message. It sounds crazy and counterintuitive to the logic of simplifying your markets, but it's key to the leverage of intellectual property. It's like the inventor who keeps finding new applications for their invention.

For this to work you have to see your expertise at a meta level and not simply at the level of technical know-how. You then need to make sure the markets are full of people you like to work with.

WORK WITH PEOPLE YOU LIKE

Our mantra is to:

> Do work you love
> with people you like
> the way you want.

This doesn't mean that you experience joy and bliss every day of your practice. It is, however, a key to what's next in your business.

The part of this mantra that relates to 'market' is the 'people you like' element. We advise thought leaders in the start-up phase of their practice to think less about this idea and more about hitting their financial targets. Generally, our advice to anyone below blue belt ($480,000 a year) is that if someone offers you money for something you do, take it. It may sound a bit mercenary, but it's necessary. Mostly, when we are helping clever people to be commercially smart, it's the commercially smart bit they need the most help with.

At some point, though, you need to assess the value of the market you serve less from a commercial point of view and more from an energetic one. Ask yourself the question: 'At the end of a day with this market, do I feel energized or depleted?' We will cover more of this in the 'Beyond black belt' chapter.

Many people say that they don't want to do business with friends. We ask, 'What's the alternative?' If you are not working with friends, what do you call the people with whom you spend most of your waking hours?

As a practice, you get to choose who you hang out with.

TWO DISTINCT MARKETS: PUBLIC OR PROFESSIONAL

The other thing to build into your 'market' thinking is the idea of two core channels: one that is public, and one that is professional. By 'public' we mean that people pay individually for what you offer and generally do so with a credit card. The 'professional' market will pay on invoice. Public is mostly about individuals, while professional is usually about entities.

EXAMPLE 1

Public

Real-estate principals who come to learn how to manage their rock star agents who might leave them. They pay $990 to attend a one-day workshop on the topic. They pay with their credit cards.

Professional

A real-estate head franchise or license group which engages you to speak 12 times on an annual agent update. They pay 12 × $5,000 and do so on invoice.

In this first example, the market is similar from an industry point of view. The difference is the relationship between them and you. In the public arena, the individuals have a direct relationship with you as individuals and a financial transaction between each of them and you occurs. In the professional arena, you are generally 'hired' by an individual on behalf of their organization and you are delivering your message to their people. Your client is the person who engaged you and, often, the participants were not involved in selecting your message.

EXAMPLE 2

Public

Teaching public-speaking skills to independent consultants who want to move from being outsourced employees to subject-matter experts. They pay as individuals to attend your six-day Speakership Program: $5,000 per head for the program.

Professional

Helping corporate leaders to understand the art of speakership — identifying the missing link between strategy and leadership. A 12-month program delivered for $5,000 a head over the 12 months. Minimum 20 people. This would be invoiced.

In this second example, the message is the constant element but the markets are clearly differentiated as public or professional.

EXAMPLE 3

Public

Helping small business owners focus on take-home versus turnover. Focusing on increasing their net worth and their external business investments.

Professional

Running an emerging leaders program throughout a public sector (government) local council group. This group hires you to deliver it to their staff.

In this third example, there is no relationship between the market or even the message. The thought leader simply has IP and capability to address the needs of both channels.

When you look at the above examples, especially the third, it's easy to see why people might fear a kind of 'scattered brand' issue. Don't worry about that. As long as you know why they make sense, then the rest is simply perception management.

MARKET NARROWLY, DELIVER BROADLY

This is a great mantra to keep in mind when marketing your practice. We have searched the Internet trying to find who first said it, and can only find general references where others use it. We don't take credit for the idea — but we see it as extremely useful to pass on.

The first part of the mantra is 'market narrowly'. When we are starting out we don't want to cut anyone out, so typically we market broadly; we cast the net wide. Unfortunately, this doesn't work — paradoxically, the more targeted and the narrower the marketing is, the more effective it becomes.

Marketing broadly is a common mistake that individuals make when they get started. A business coach will often help small to medium businesses and will market his or her ability to work with all of them. The problem is that there are lots of other business coaches out there doing the same thing — and there is no way to differentiate your offer from everyone else's.

If, however, this business coach specialized in helping bookkeepers grow their bookkeeping business, they would definitely stand out from the hundreds of other business coaches. This approach also allows the specialized business coach to gather stronger referrals, because a bookkeeper will be much more likely to take a call from someone with expertise helping bookkeepers than with other businesses.

Just about everyone we come across who is starting out (and many who are a fair way down the track) don't market narrowly enough. So what happens if someone knocks on your door and wants to do business with you, but doesn't fit your niche? Do you say no to the business?

In the early days, you say 'yes, thank you' and improve your delivery modes whilst getting paid. Just don't talk about it; don't add it to your marketing. Don't make the mistake of letting some current but otherwise 'non-representative' activity define your future positioning.

If you find that the work is sweet, though, and you have a lot to share in the new area, then get on and create a new cluster and incorporate it into your practice game plan.

THE POWER OF POSITIONING

How easy is it for you to get clients, and does it get easier over time?

In a traditional business model, *marketing* is the key to creating new interest. Once that interest has been generated, you then move onto *sales*. A formal and systematic sales process then creates new business. Over time you then work on existing *relationships* and begin to create more business from that already existing. Classic business coaches will tell you that it is easier to hold on to and service an existing customer than it is to get new customers. These three strategies are Business 101 — nothing new. If you market, sell and build relationships, you will drive growth through your business. They require you to push your value proposition out into the world. This is the work of getting business.

For many service-based professionals, the idea of selling is completely alien. They will tell you, often proudly, that they have never had to sell a day in their life. This is because they rely on reputation to grow their business. Their business is a referral business. This is super-powerful, trumps formal marketing and selling, and takes relationship-building to a whole new level. Basically, your awesome work creates more awesome work.

Referrals are great; recommendations are even better. A recommendation occurs when your clients or business network members take an active role in you getting business. The difference is that a referral is passive, e.g. 'You should work with Scott Stein', while a recommendation is active, e.g. 'Let me call Scott now and see when he can see you to discuss this.' This then leads on to the idea of *positioning*. When you are positioned as a thought leader in your field, everything gets easier. Referrals, recommendations and positioning make growing your business almost effortless. When you get these dynamics working in your business, you begin to leverage reputation to pull business in the door.

If you review the expert to authority model below, you can see this idea visually. The numbers alongside the stages are indicative of how effective each stage is at getting you business when compared with someone who does none of these things. So, positioning your-self as a thought leader will get you ten times more business when compared to someone who is not using any of these strategies.

EXPERT TO AUTHORITY MODEL

PULL	positioning	10x
	recommendation	8x
	referral	6x
PUSH	relationships	4x
	sales	3x
	marketing	2x

There is a turning point when you move from being an expert to being an authority, often around the blue-belt level; when you move from *knowing something* to *being known for knowing something*. At this point the game has changed! It's now easier to get clients and charge a premium for your time. You have gone from pushing to get work to having the luxury to pick and choose the work you do. You now need to become very discerning about whether the activity you undertake is going to add to or detract from your positioning.

THE EVOLUTION OF SALES

Sales 101 is basically about selling techniques. It becomes a numbers game: see enough people and get good enough at the techniques, and people will buy what you have to sell. The principle behind Sales 101 is *some will, some won't; so what? Get on with it!*

Sales 201 is basically about relationship selling: get to know me well enough and build enough shared experience with me, and it's likely I will do business with you. The principle behind Sales 201 is that *people do business with people they like.*

Sales 301 is basically about diagnostic selling: ask enough questions and understand enough about people's buying criteria, and you can create a proposition that gets you the business. The principle behind diagnostic selling is *understand me, show me you get it, and we will do business.*

For thought leaders selling their thoughts, each type of sales approach will work. So don't worry if you have capabilities at any of the three stages. It's all good and it will help you do more business.

However, in each of these first three sales approaches, you are in effect convincing the client to do business with you. We reckon that when you are the thing being sold, this gets weird. It kind of gets personal. It's also not the way a brain surgeon sells. What you need to do is switch from convincing others, and rather, to stand in your conviction around what you know and why others should care. As such, we think you need to move on to the next evolution of sales.

Sales 401 is all about authority selling: you know something and others might just have a need that you have already nailed a solution for. It's about you disclosing your expertise first and asserting a level of knowledge on how to fix key issues that people may be experiencing, rather than assessing their level of need and creating a proposal (diagnostic selling). The principle behind authority selling is *I know what's going on and can help you with that.*

We call it 'clicking', and in essence it's about linking known problems that your target market expresses often with the intellectual property you know can help them. Problem-bridging is the big idea. Below is a quick overview.

CLICKING MODEL

COMPASSION		CREDIBILITY		CONVICTION	
1	2	3	4	5	6
Known spoken	Known unspoken	Value model	IP snapshot	Invite	Commit

PROBLEM-BRIDGING

Step 1: Establish their known, spoken problems

This will be the problem that people openly discuss, and believe that to date no one has come up with a solution for. The fact that these concerns are blatant and openly spoken of is a positive. It gives you a bridge anchor point into their predominant dialogue.

It might be helpful to imagine what the conversation would be if you put 100 of your target market in a room and asked them to share their biggest challenge. What would they say? What keeps them awake at night? What is their primary concern?

Step 2: Identify their known, unspoken problems

These are the problems that your target market knows, but won't speak up about. What do they really think about, when they are sitting quietly pondering their situation? They understand the problems but may not have voiced them yet, either to themselves or others. This is the problem that you don't have to dig too deeply beneath the surface to uncover.

In this case, ask yourself what they would say if sitting with you at the end of a long day, with half a bottle of good red down. The unspoken problems are typically personal fears and concerns; doubt often creeps in here.

Step 3: Draw a value model

A value model is a contextual diagram you can draw to explain the placement of your ideas in the context of the person's situation. It's nice to have a metaphor up your sleeve to go with the model. A value model is simply the *Why* piece (we call this a Green Sheet) to your *How* pieces (IP Snapshots).

Often experts want to solve problems straightaway. They are so into their ideas that they throw them away on ears that are either not interested or don't know why they should be interested. The three problems described in this section (the last one is explained below) and a value model fix that.

To see the poster-child version of a value model, let's look at the 'white to black belt' growth model that this book and the Thought Leaders program is based on. The model is repeated on the next page.

BELT	INCOME	FOCUS
5th Dan	$1,200,000	Distribution
4th Dan	$1,080,000	Capacity
3rd Dan	$960,000	Productivity
2nd Dan	$840,000	Engagement
Black Belt	$720,000	Investment
Red Belt	$600,000	Leverage
Blue Belt	$480,000	Positioning
Green Belt	$360,000	Activity
Yellow Belt	$240,000	Value
White Belt	$120,000	Decision

There are three key elements that need to be on a value model:

- Currency

- Aspiration

- Location

Let's walk through each in turn.

Currency

A great value model has a currency that others will value. This can be money; but it could equally be time, energy or some other quantifiable outcome.

Aspiration

A great value model has a sense of compelling future. It should show how to take your ideas to get somewhere better. It should mobilize in pursuit of a better future. On the Thought Leaders Revenue Ladder, you see that an infopreneur can move from white belt to black belt on the ladder. We also believe the 'sweet spot' is located just above blue belt, where your referrals are creating most of your new business.

Location

Finally, a great value model is one where you can see where you are on the journey. You need to be able to locate where you are on your model. In the Thought Leaders Revenue Ladder, individuals can say 'This is where I am at the moment and this is where I would love to get to.' When people can locate themselves on a model, it is easy to identify where they want to go and how you can work with them to achieve this outcome.

Value models are essentially helping people with three issues:

- Where am I on this journey? (Location)

- Where do I want to go next? (Aspiration)

- And what do I value most? (Currency)

Step 4:   Tell them their unknown, unspoken problems (essentially, one of your IP Snapshots)

The unknown problem is the most dangerous of all the problems, but also the most powerful. If you don't get this right and you express it as true, you have lost any chance of getting your idea off the ground. If you get it right, though, you will see a light come on in your client's eyes. They will nod as they get to see you put form around something they have known to be true but have not been able to name or identify. If you are the person who does this for someone else, you become the trusted advisor and a partner for life.

Once you have your value model drawn, you then simply want to invite them to work with you and secure a commitment.

In most cases this fourth step is about introducing a piece of IP, an IP Snapshot, that serves as a quick introduction to *How* people go about getting the currency of worth shown in your value model.

Step 5: Make a clear invitation

Although this seems obvious, you'd be surprised at how many people completely leave this out. It's no use having a great conversation, and not inviting anyone to sign up for your programs. It's no use taking your prospect through the first four steps in a meeting, then shaking their hand and walking out. Yet that's what so many people do!

It's absolutely vital that you make an invitation. Lay it on the table, make it clear what's involved, and allow them the space to answer. You need to communicate what it'll look like if you work together. Maybe it's "I'll run a workshop on this date, and it'll cost this much money" or it might be "I'll deliver a coaching program that runs over this many sessions, starts in two weeks, and you pay this way." Whatever it is, they need to understand exactly what you're offering, and be given the chance to say yes.

Step 6: Follow through on the answer

If somebody says yes, it's time to actually get payment, a deposit, or issue an invoice. If the yes is part of a bigger project, set up the next step in the process such as putting a date in your diaries for the next meeting, scheduling the first coaching session, or agreeing on the next part of the engagement. We'll look at this in more detail in chapter 8.

If the answer is no, that's fine. We are not attached to the result, and they may not need our offering at this time. If appropriate, refer them to another thought leader who may be better suited to their current needs. Let them know that they are welcome to approach you again in the future when they're in a better position to take on your services. They may still be a future customer.

8.

Selling Thought Leadership

You don't close a sale, you open a relationship if you want to build a long-term, successful enterprise.

— PATRICIA FRIPP

There are a couple of myths that we want to dispel about selling your thought leadership.

The first is that you can get someone else to do it for you. Lots of people say to us that they love doing the thinking and the delivery … but the selling, not so much. There are many Thought leaders who would happily run workshops and coaching programs every day, if only they could find someone else to sell it for them.

We have never, ever seen that work in a thought leaders practice. Your job as a thought leader is to think, *sell*, and deliver. No one else can sell your IP and your programs better than you, and employing a sales rep or a business development manager just doesn't work in this model. Sorry.

The second myth is build it and they will come. We have this fantasy that once we've written the book or built the website or spoken at *the* conference then we just have to sit back and wait for the phone to ring. Maybe, after you've been running a cluster for a decade, and you have a list of 1500 engaged folk in that market opening your newsletter, then just for that cluster it might start to sell itself. But for everything else your job is to go and sell and your stuff. Face to face and belly to belly.

However there is good news too. If you use the following approach it's not going to feel like sales. Even though you will be having sales meetings with the intent to transact, it will feel like service. This process looks at how to manage a sales meeting powerfully and respectfully in a way that contributes to your prospect whether or not they choose to do business with you.

	BEFORE	DURING	DECISION POINT
MINDSET	**Cool** *It's a numbers game*	**Selective** *Choose your clients*	**Reverent** *This is a sacred moment*
ENERGY	**Sold** *You be convinced*	**Dance** *Be present and joyous*	**Surrended** *Don't be attached*
CONVERSATION	**Clean** *Be upfront*	**Clicking** *Know the world*	**Invitation** *Put it out there*

We want to develop the right thinking (mindset), what you need to say (conversation), and the right tone (energetic state) for each and every selling conversation. This applies to each stage of the conversation: before (what happens prior to the sales meeting), during (the body of the meeting), and at the decision point (the end of the conversation where the prospect is choosing whether or not to do business with you).

Strangely enough we believe that the first stage is the most important. What happens before you get into the room with a prospect has more bearing on the outcome than what you say during the meeting, or how you ask for the business (although obviously these things matter too). But unfortunately most sales training focuses on what happens during the meeting and at the close.

Likewise we believe that your mindset and your energetic state is every bit as important as what you say, even though most sales theory is only about what you say. As you can see, the model explores all three aspects (mindset, energy and conversation) before the meeting, during the meeting and at the decision point.

COOL

The mindset we want before a sales conversation is to be cool, recognizing that sales is a numbers game. When people are weak at sales and not powerful with commercial conversations, it generally comes back to a fear of rejection. Anyone with self worth issues (which is just about everyone on the planet) risks mistaking rejection in a sales meeting with personal rejection. Instead of understanding that the prospect is saying no to the cluster we're selling, at some level we interpret the 'no' as a saying no to us, to rejecting us.

Thinking about sales as a numbers games helps eliminate that. There is an expected conversion rate. We know that some people will say yes, some will say no, and that's the game. There is an old Amway saying that encapsulates this: 'Some will, some won't, so what'. And while we don't love everything about Amway, there is definitely wisdom in this.

Trains in Singapore run a bit differently to the way they do in many parts of the world. In Singapore there is a train every three or four minutes, so you never have to look at a timetable. And you never run for a train. It's too hot and — importantly — you know that there is another train coming. It doesn't matter if you miss this one.

We want to be like that with our sales meeting—to be cool. Because it's a numbers game, we understand our conversion ratios and how many meetings we need to have to hit our targets. If we have ten sales meetings lined up, we aren't desperate to close any of them. There is always another train coming.

The conversion rate depends on the size of opportunity, the previous relationship, and a number of other factors. However, as a starting point, with any new cluster that we launch we factor in a one-in-four conversion rate. In other words we are aiming to make a sale in 25% of our sales meetings. So if we had a $3,000 program, and we wanted to make $120,000 from that product in a year, obviously we would need to sell 40 of them. If our conversion rate is one in four, we would need 160 meetings. The game is then to set up 160 meetings, get 40 people to say yes and 120 to say no.

Going into a meeting knowing that it is a numbers game, and that the aim is to get to a yes or a no without much attachment to which, lets us be much lighter in the meeting. And as we'll see, it helps us be surrendered at the decision point.

SOLD

Stephen Covey says that every project is created twice: first in your mind, then in reality. Similarly, every sale is made twice: first to yourself, and then to the prospect.

If you aren't sold yourself, you're not ready to have a sales meeting. You need to go back to work on your product or your offer until you're in love with it. You know you are sold when you almost wish that you were a customer just so you could get what it is that you're selling.

It bears repeating—the first sale is *always* to yourself. If you are not sold, no one else will be. Your work before the sales meeting is to make sure that you are sold, energetically, so that you are convinced that what you are selling is going to provide value to the right client. You need to be very clear that ultimately the customer chooses whether the sale occurs or not. Your job is simply to ensure the right customers are given the option of saying 'yes' or 'no' to your program.

A thought leaders approach is: *'This is what I know, and I help these sort of people, who are experiencing these problems to get these results. If that's of interest to you, it would be an honour to work together.'*

Before going into a sales meeting there needs to be absolutely no doubt in your mind that if the person in front of you is one of those people, facing those problems and looking for those results, then it would be really smart for them to work with you. The prospect is always looking for certainty, and your certainty makes it safe for them to buy.

Ironically, if you are convinced, you don't need to convince the prospect. When you have certainty, the person in front of you won't need to be convinced — that will happen automatically. And if you find yourself having lots of conversations where you are trying to convince the prospect about the value of your offering, it's a sign that you aren't sold yourself — that there is still work to do here.

The key to your conviction is your IP Snapshots. When you have done the thinking, *really* done the thinking, and captured it properly, something powerful happens. If you're not sold on your cluster, keep working on your IP Snapshots until you are.

Effective sales conversations happen when your heart, your mind and your mouth are all saying the same thing — and this only comes from a deep conviction. We've all had the experience of being sold to by someone who isn't sold themselves, and doesn't have that congruence. We can feel it — and if you are conflicted about what you are selling the people you are talking to can feel it too.

The beauty of this is that when you are sold, sales actually becomes an act of service. You begin to feel as if your offerings are the commercial equivalent to a first aid kit and you are happy to offer its contents to anyone who is in pain or need. So instead of trying to convince people about what you have, you can serve them by helping them determine if what you have will make their life better. It's almost as if instead of sitting across from them you move round and sit beside them — you are on their side.

CLEAN

There is nothing worse than going to catch up with someone, or showing up at a social function, only to find out that there was a hidden agenda to sell something. Imagine being invited to a dinner party only to be offered a great '*business opportunity*' in a multi-level marketing business or a timeshare resort. It's a nightmare, and many of us have lived it.

And unfortunately, when we're not *clean* with our setup, this is exactly what we are doing to our prospects. Perhaps not quite as badly as the example above, but it's definitely in the same spectrum. Too many people will set up a sales meeting with a loose invitation to catch up for a coffee. The meeting won't be powerful and will feel sleazy. You know you are there to sell something, but can't be too overt about it because the meeting's intent wasn't set up properly. The sales part of the conversation will be weak, and the experience won't be great for either of you.

You'll end up catching up for half an hour, talking briefly about what you actually want to sell, and not getting to the invitation, let alone to a decision.

The conversation before the actual meeting needs to be a clean set up. Be upfront and transparent about what the meeting is about. If the purpose of the meeting is to tell the prospect about what you are offering, to find out if they need it and to make a commercial offer, make sure that you communicate that. Both parties need to know beforehand what is on the agenda.

A clean setup makes everything else much more powerful. First, it means that if the offer isn't relevant, or of interest, you don't have to waste an hour of both your lives finding out. More people will knock back the meeting… but that's a good thing. You'll only meet with people who are interested, and your conversion rate will improve.

This also means that when you get together, you can get right into it. You can spend the time productively and get to a decision point in one meeting. And you won't damage your relationships by trying to sell something when it's not expected and feels inappropriate.

So if you want to meet Mary to tell her about a program you are selling, a great setup could be something like: *"Hi Mary, I've got this workshop coming up on such and such date, that's all about achieving these sort of results. I thought of you, and wanted to make a time to catch up and explore if this is something that is going to be of value to you."* Upfront and clean.

SELECTIVE

During the meeting the most powerful mindset is *selective* — be very clear that you are choosing your clients. Get clear before you meet about what type of people you want to work with, what sort of work you do, and how you want to work.

Our friend Bianca runs a bed and breakfast in Singapore, and uses AirBnB to rent out some rooms in her house. She rejects 40% of the people who want to stay with her. 40% ! Four out of every ten people who fill in the form online, enter their credit card and are ready to pay, she says no to.

How cool is that? Her whole attitude is that if people are staying in her house, she wants to enjoy the experience. If someone sent her an email that just says "We need a room for two people", she knows that they are not her sort of people. It isn't friendly, as she says, it's the sort of request you make to a hotel, not a home stay. So she says no. And she trusts her intuition.

One of our mantras is to do work you love with people you like the way you want. Bianca is the personification of this — she only wants to do business with people she likes.

So when you go into a sales meeting, make sure you are choosing your clients. Have part of your sales system be the point where *you* choose. Have a strategy for rejecting the clients who aren't a fit.

We promise you two things will happen. Life will get better as you do more work with people you like. And paradoxically, you will become more effective at selling as you become more attractive. Notice your reaction when we shared that Bianca rejects 40% of requests — didn't that make her more attractive? Part of you wanted to be in the 60%. The same will happen with you when you choose your clients, and more importantly, are willing to say no to the ones you don't choose.

During the meeting you are interviewing the prospect just as much as they are interviewing you. You are determining if they are someone that you can help, that you would want to serve, and that you would enjoy hanging out with. If not, be prepared to walk away. Paradoxically, if this is authentic it makes you much more attractive. If it is clear that you won't just work with anyone and there is a bar that the prospect has to reach to become your client, working with you becomes more attractive. However, this has to be authentic — please don't do this as a sales technique.

We ask ourselves three things before we take on a client. First, can we get excited by their vision by and what they are up to in their business? Second, do we want to hang out with them, are they someone we would like to catch up with for a coffee? And finally, can we make a significant, strategic contribution? If we don't say yes to all three, then we won't take on the client, and we will recommend that they find someone else who is a better fit.

Our good friend Michael Port writes about this in *Book Yourself Solid*. He calls it the 'red velvet rope policy' — and paints a beautiful metaphor of a red velvet rope stretched between shiny brass polls with an attendant only letting the privileged few through. He argues that choosing your clients means that you'll work with clients that you love, that you'll love every minute of it, and that you'll do your best work. Michael Port lists the following benefits of having a red velvet rope policy (and we agree):

- You'll have clean energy to do your best work.

- You'll feel invigorated and inspired.

- You'll connect with clients on a deeper level.

- You'll feel successful and confident.

- You'll know your work matters and is changing lives.

- The magic of you will come to life!

Choosing your clients is easy to say, and easy to agree with in principle, but it takes incredible courage to implement it in practice. Particularly before you are fully booked up, and when it feels like you need the money, or you need the sale. But it's worth it. All three authors have had the experience of taking on clients who weren't right, and who our intuition told us not to work with, and always ended up paying for it one way or another. Please learn from our mistakes, and select the clients that you will do your best work with.

DANCE

During the sales conversation the energy is that of a *dance*. While you have prepared what you are going to say about how you work, the problems you solve and what your great thinking is, you can't recite this like a written speech. The 'clicking' process described below will lay out the content and structure of the sales conversation, but this definitely should not be followed by rote.

You need to dance with the energy of the conversation, play with how much to intervene, what advice or mentoring to give, and how deep to go how quickly. Have fun with it. Be present and be joyous with it. There might be times where you would ask permission to give some mentoring or coaching, or say 'If we were working together, this is what I would do'. If you are in the business of giving advice, then give some in the meeting.

One of our intents for any sales meeting is that the prospect walks away having received incredible value, whether or not they buy from us. This does two things. First, it means that in the future, if circumstances change and the time is right for them, they are much more likely to come back to you and become a client at that point. Second, they will tell their friends and refer business to you, even if they aren't a client themselves. So use the opportunity to make the biggest contribution that you can.

Part of being present and *dancing* is being authentically you. Be real and authentic, and that way you are much more likely to get to know the prospect and to discover if they are somebody that you would enjoy working with.

Even if it's just an hour, it's still an hour of your life, and an hour you are spending with another human being — so be real and enjoy it. And even if it doesn't result in a sale now, make sure that it makes a difference.

CLICKING

The conversation to have during the sales meeting is a *clicking* process. Conviction selling isn't diagnostic selling. You don't go into the meeting trying to find out what's happening in their world, you go in already having a hypothesis about what their problems are and how you can solve them. You have to know their world to have the right to be selling to them in the first place. If you don't know any CEOs, you've never been a CEO and you've never worked with a CEO, you won't be able to click with a CEO and you shouldn't be selling to them. What you say in the meeting is an extended version of *'I work with these sorts of people, facing these sorts of problems, and I solve this with these ideas, which makes these results possible.'* It's the conversation we outlined in the previous chapter.

REVERENT

The mindset to hold at the decision point is one of *reverence*. This is the time when the prospect is choosing whether or not they are going to work with you. The whole purpose of getting together, and everything that has gone before, is to get to this point.

It is like they have come to a fork in the road, and two possible futures are opening up in front of them. The prospect is deciding which fork they are going to take — which future they are going to live into. We think of it a bit like the movie *Sliding Doors* with Gwyneth Paltrow. The movie follows two possible futures as she either just catches a train, or just misses it. The name of the movie comes from the moment when the two futures split, when the doors on the train slide closed and she either catches it or she doesn't.

The decision point is like that — the two possible futures split at this point in time. It is a sacred moment, and we want to treat it like that.

While we don't want to get too significant about it all, we want to hand this moment over to the prospect with due reverence, and allow them to make their decision. In *Fierce Conversations*, Susan Scott recommends that we let "silence do the heavy lifting". This is great advice for how to give this moment its due reverence. Once you make the invitation, be quiet. Give this moment to the prospect like a gift, and then stop talking.

The ancient Greeks used two words for time, *Chronos* and *Kairos*. The former, *Chronos,* is the closest to our sense of time in English. It refers to sequential time — the passing of minutes, hours and days. The latter, *Kairos,* signifies a time in between — those instants when opportunity presents, when something special is about to happen. What we sometimes call critical moments. Mostly when we think about time management, productivity, efficiency and effectiveness, we are talking about using chronological time better. Generally we don't pay enough attention to *Kairos,* those critical moments upon which everything turns. The decision point of the meeting is potentially one of these *Kairos* moments for our prospects. Giving it due reverence means treating it as such.

SURRENDERED

Your energy at this point is *surrendered,* allowing the prospect to make their decision. You are not attached to the outcome. You have handed over the moment to the client and are unattached.

You might want to work together, but you don't need to. And there is a world of difference between the two.

We've all had the experience of being sold to by someone who was attached to the result. They needed the money, or they had a sales target they needed to hit. That desperation comes out through their pores, and we want to run a mile. And most of us at some point have been there too, we are behind on our sales targets, or there is no money in the bank and there are bills to pay. Suddenly we are attached, and it really feels like we *need* this client.

Somehow we need to interrupt this state and lose our attachment. Your energy, your being at this point, needs to be that you are fine either way. You are OK, whether or not the prospect chooses to do business with you. And if you think about it, of course you are. Your survival never depends on one customer, even though it might feel like it.

This is linked to your mindset from before the meeting, to knowing that it is a numbers game. That the objective of the meeting is to get to a 'yes' or a 'no'. That's it. And the yes or the no is not *your* yes or no. The yes or the no decision is the customer's alone. Remember that your job is simply to ensure that they have the opportunity to make that decision. We love this as it takes all the pressure associated with traditional sales methods and dissolves the pressure allowing a calm neutrality to pervade your mind and body. The customer will feel, see, and hear how relaxed you are and feel better placed to make the right decision for themselves. Allowing them to choose without pressure is in itself a service.

So, whilst you would love to work together, you are going to be fine either way. At one level, you don't even care what they choose, you'll both be fine either way. After all, how can you be upset with someone else choosing what is best for them?

Only the selfish are ever upset by customers choosing what is best for their situation.

A useful belief to support you in staying surrendered is to acknowledge that you cannot chose another soul's journey. And while we don't actually believe our lives are pre-determined, that can be a useful delusion to hold during a sales meeting. Pretend that the outcome of the meeting is already determined and that you are just getting together with the prospect to find out what it is. That positive delusion helps you resist attachment.

Michael Port gives us another useful perspective to help break our attachment. He says that there are people we are meant to serve, and people we are not meant to serve. Being surrendered means trusting this — trusting that we will end up working with the people we are meant to serve. And either we won't choose the people we are not meant to serve, or they won't choose us. In other words, when someone says no, that is a good thing, because at least for now they are not someone we are meant to serve.

The beautiful thing about being detached is that you can be much stronger in the conversation without it feeling like pressure. When you are attached to an outcome you end up walking on egg shells because the energy isn't clean, and it can end up feeling manipulative or pressured. When you are truly surrendered you can express yourself fully, say exactly what you think, recommend whatever you want and still leave the prospect completely free to choose either way. Again, its a beautiful gift to give — a way of being at service during the sales process.

INVITATION

It is almost criminal to get to the end of the conversation and not make the invitation. We see it happen all the time where a prospect is ready to buy, but instead of making the invitation the thought leader says: *"Get back to me"*, or *"I'll be in touch"*, or *"Let's email about what's next"*. DON'T DO THAT! You are ripping off your prospect. You've brought them to the brink, you've shown them a new possibility, a different future, and then you've yanked it away from them.

If we liken your cluster to a first aid kit, to not ask the customer if they would like the bandage, the pain killer or the antiseptic, is bordering on cruelty. You have the solution, they can certainly see and feel the benefits of your offering, but at the last moment you withhold the chance for them to access your solution.

If you have something of value, something that could change this person's life, that could make their world better, and you've both spent an hour with the express purpose of determining whether this is for them, and you want to work with them — ask for the business! Make the invitation. If you don't, you have wasted both your time and theirs.

Most of the time they are ready to make a decision at this point. They have spent quality time getting to know you, getting a sense of if they want to work with you, exploring the value they would get and how things would change. If you leave without them making a decision, nothing has changed in their world. And the decision about whether to work with you or not is still in their future, not in their past.

However, if they have bought what it is you are selling, their world is already different. Even if they have bought a program that is in the future, the commitment they have made changes everything. They are living into a different future. We have all had the experience of selling mentoring programs to clients and having them show up to the first session already having produced breakthrough results. The program begins when the client commits.

It also makes your life much easier. If you don't make the invitation, you'll have to follow up, have another conversation, and begin to enrol them again. You will lose sales that you otherwise would have made, and not be able to serve people that you should be working with.

If your cluster is a big ticket item — lets say a $100k 12 month engagement into a large organisation — it may take more than one meeting to close the deal. In that case the invitation is for the next meeting, or the next step, whatever that may be. However the same principles apply — keep progressing the sale.

As we said earlier, the reason we don't make the invitation is that we are scared of rejection. At an unconscious level we fear being told no. We are tribal animals, and for hundreds of thousands of years our survival has depended upon us being accepted by our tribes, so we are wired to avoid rejection. However, if you are in the game of sales, you need to get over this. You move from a sense of survival to a sense of service. Shift from *'fight and flight'* to *'light and alright'*.

Do whatever work you need to do so that you are OK with people saying no to you in a sales meeting. Part of this is recognising that when someone says no to your offering they are not rejecting you personally (although this is a bit more challenging when you are selling yourself). However part of it runs deeper than this.

Of course, you are being selective and choosing your clients, so if this isn't someone you want to work with, don't make the invitation. However, if you do want to work with them, and they meet your criteria, tell them so and make the invitation. Tell them how you could work together, what it will cost, and ask them if they want to go ahead and work with you.

If they say yes, secure the commitment (either take a payment or send an invoice depending on the client and the type of work). And if they say no, make sure you thank them for the opportunity to share your offering and have some other system for staying in touch and nurturing the relationship so that they will come back to you when the time is right.

9.

Power of Positioning

What helps people, helps business.

— Leo Burnett

'*So what do you do?*'

This is one of the most common questions asked when someone meets another person for the first time. For most people, a simple job title is the most common response, which unfortunately leaves little positive impression in the recipient's mind. However, when you come into contact with a thought leader they have a particular gleam in their eye and their response is quite often inspiring. It is not that they are enthusiastic and over the top, it is just as if they have found a secret formula that positions them as an expert — someone that others want to find out more about. Even further, the thought leaders that have really worked on their positioning provide you with something that you can easily repeat to others — further enhancing their brand, reputation and capabilities.

The process we unpack in this chapter is called the Positioning Matrix. The process is built around the nine steps of positioning who you are and what you do. The Positioning Matrix is a process and discipline every thought leader should develop. With a little preparation and practice of this process you will quickly learn how to communicate your ideas in a way that captures the attention of others and is rigidly flexible. That sounds like a contradiction in terms, doesn't it? Bear with us: you'll soon see what we mean.

This process was created to help people share sentences that introduce themselves and their ideas in an elegant, effective and quick fashion.

You can apply this process in initial networking greetings, simple corridor conversations and inflight introductions, right through to formal proposals that outline your ideas or in high-stakes presentations delivered to introduce or gain acceptance of your big ideas.

There's a paradox in positioning — that we are not what we do, yet as thought leaders we still need to be able to answer the question 'What do you do?' in a way that makes us better known and creates interest. Many card-carrying introverts find the prospect of commercial networking about as attractive as having root-canal treatment. Still, we recognize that without sharing our expertise with staff, customers, clients and attendees, no one besides us will know our thought leadership.

THE POSITIONING MATRIX

This nine-step positioning process achieves two things: first, it enables you to consistently answer the question 'What do you do?' with an appropriate level of detail. And, second, it enables you to create a flexible positioning statement that can be creatively applied to any introduction situation.

It has been said that we all need a good 'elevator statement', a succinct 30-second sales pitch or service position that creates awareness about what we do and how it is unique or valuable. And while we don't remember a time when we successfully did business in an elevator, we do agree that we all need a way to efficiently answer the question 'What do you do?' so that we are positioned as 'top of mind' should our customer ever face a situation where they need our products or services. To approach the way we answer the question 'What do you do?' with a level of creativity, intelligence and purpose (sadly lacking in most introductions), we need to think about a number of different things.

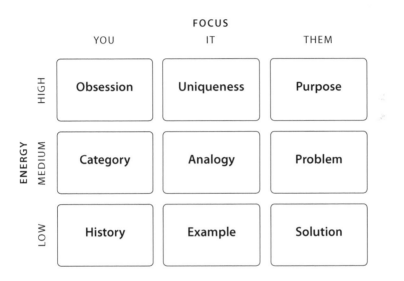

The focus levels

If you explore the way people introduce themselves, you will notice patterns emerging. The first pattern that becomes clear is the focus of the introduction. The three options for focus are: to focus on *You*, to focus on *It*, or to focus on *Them*.

- *You* is obviously all about you — who you are, what you have done, and what you are into.

- *It* is all about the activity — examples of how it has worked for someone, what it is like and maybe a few good stories about what it is that you do.

- *Them* is all about the outcomes that your customers and clients achieve — you may ask questions, identify the key challenges they face or even get into solutions.

While there are no hard and fast rules for which to use when, we find that the more intimate the situation, the more appropriate it is to answer the question with a focus on *You*. If you're unsure of who it is you are in front of or talking to, you may focus on the activity that you perform, the *It*. If the person you are speaking to is a client or employee, then you could focus on the outcome, the *Them*.

Here are some examples of how you might change the focus based on the environment.

Situation focus:

- Dinner party: Personal *You*

- Networking event: Activity *It*

- Prospect's boardroom: Outcomes *Them*

Of course, it may work to your advantage to juxtapose the focus — when you are versed in the nine positioning channels you can pick and choose your way around the grid as the situation dictates.

The energy levels

The second pattern that emerges in introduction situations is the energetic intensity of the introduction. There are three energy levels: *Low, Medium* and *High*. Certain situations lend themselves to a more energetic and passionate introduction than others. Of course, some would argue that the higher the energy, the greater the impact on the other person — we don't agree. The key is to respond at the appropriate intensity, and rise to the higher levels if the listener is receptive.

Take the person sitting next to you on an eight-hour flight. We don't know about you but we don't want a 'pushy networking superstar' in seat 24A wowing us with her high-energy elevator statement. In this situation, a *Low* energy introduction that grows in intensity as your interest grows may be more effective.

Combining the patterns of *Focus* and *Energy*, with their three options each, gives us the nine different channels of introduction.

History

This is basically a verbal résumé outlining where you have been and what you have done. Be sure to edit out the irrelevant stuff. We learn to write résumés when we are young and before we've done anything. As a result we tend to pad them out, making as much as possible out of little. Now that you are a little older you can drop the stuff that you did years ago, or at least just sketch out the details. Only say that which is useful. For example:

> *I grew up in Newcastle, moved to Sydney to study, graduated in the late eighties and went to work in a prison. I then worked for the Australian Council for Health and Lend Lease, wrote a few books and ended up here on the corporate speaking circuit.*

Category

The category channel is intentionally lacking in creativity. This is a black-and-white answer to the question. We often use this one as a trial balloon to see how interested the person asking the question is. You would answer with a professional category.

> *I am a speaker.*

> *I am the senior tax partner for a multinational professional services firm.*

> *I am a strategic communications consultant.*

> *I am a coach.*

Obsession

Most of the time, you won't get a chance to speak about your obsession. Certainly not before carefully building up to that point. When the opportunity does present itself, however, you get the privilege of sharing your passion. It's your chance to really express why you do what you do. This is the time to get fired up about what you believe, and expose the intensity of your inner drive.

> *I know that CEOs should spend less time preparing speeches and more time running businesses. Too many great leaders fail to think before they speak. If they simply got their ideas down more effectively they would make a greater impact when they spoke.*
>
> *We're surrounded by so many productivity tools which we don't use productively! I think organizations would be so much more effective if they implemented some basic IT training.*

Example

Choose an appropriate client case study, an example of someone you have been working with recently. You're aiming to demonstrate the nature of your activity and who it serves. You want to aim to make this example relevant to the person in front of you (to the best of your knowledge), and not one that may jeopardize your chances of working with their organization. For example, if you were selling to a particular bank, you probably don't want to use a case study from a competitor of theirs!

> *One client we worked with recently had a problem getting their internal sales team to move from a product-based selling process into a relationship-based environment. Over six months we moved the incentive schemes and culture from having a focus on transactions to having a focus on relationships. They noticed a 40 per cent positive shift in client retention,*

and this looks like impacting the profit positively by another $250,000 this
quarter alone.

Analogy

This channel is particularly useful if you sell an intangible service or a
new category of product or service. You draw a comparison between
an already established concept and what you do. This enables the
listener to quickly understand your concept inside the framework of
something that is already familiar to them.

> *We are like a sports management company for information experts.*

> *I'm like a car mechanic for your computer. I'll check your system and give*
> *you a warrant of fitness.*

> *I'm like the boarding announcer for a flight at the airport. I tell you when*
> *to get on board and invest, and when to wait patiently.*

Uniqueness

Here, you try to set yourself apart from others in your field. This
is where you get to state your unique selling proposition and make
a distinction between yourself and others. Whatever the masses
are doing, try to position some part of what you do as contrary or
opposed to this.

> *While I am a lawyer, I am also a chartered accountant. This means we*
> *can handle all parts of the deal for you. We find this saves our clients time*
> *and money.*

> *I'm a business consultant, but I have worked in Japan for 14 years so have*
> *contacts there and I speak the language.*

Solution

This is similar to a case study or example, but here you actually state the benefits you create for others. It's often easy to ask a question that explains why you have created a certain solution.

> *Do you find that you are spending too much time stuck in the day-to-day running of your business? We have created a personal effectiveness system that allows most people to get more done in less time. Our average client finds an extra three days productivity per month when using our system.*

Problem

A problem is best described as the day-to-day internal dialogue your prospect has around what they do. When you start speaking about what's already on their mind they truly engage with your products and services. Their realization that you know their problems, and that you know how to solve them, is a powerful tool for you.

> *The biggest problems in any law firm are keeping good staff, and moving from a fee-for-service model to a value-based advice model. Our business addresses these problems and creates a future-proof environment for any mid-sized law firm to grow.*

Purpose

This is where you express the client's reason for being in a way that shows you are aligned. You express how what you do is a perfect fit for their purpose. If you can summarize their goals while describing the way you will help them achieve them, your prospect will gain a lot of confidence in your understanding of their overall purpose.

> *Here at Cocktail Capers we realize that you should have as much fun at your own party as you would at someone else's. That's why we take care*

of everything from start to finish. You get to feel like you can just go to sleep at the end of the evening and know that when you wake up the next morning it's as if the party was held somewhere else.

POSITIONING MATRIX STARTERS

STEP	STARTER SENTENCE
1. History	*I began 10 years ago … Then five years ago … For the last year I've been working on …*
2. Category	*I consider myself a …*
3. Obsession	*What I'm really passionate about is …*
4. Example	*Just the other day I/we …*
5. Analogy	*It's kind of like the [x] for [x] …*
6. Uniqueness	*The thing that's different about us/our process is …*
7. Solution	*Some of the things we've been able to do include …*
8. Problem	*The way I see it, there are three big challenges for the people I help …*
9. Purpose	*In my opinion, I feel that you're in the business of …*

There's no doubt that there are more ways that we could use to introduce ourselves, but these nine channels are an excellent starter's guide to enable you to introduce yourself powerfully in any situation. Take some time to follow the various pathways you might take while talking with a person for the first time. It may help to read back through the nine examples that we have just provided to better understand how they all fit together in the matrix.

Your Method

10.

Diversifying Delivery Modes

To the man who only has a hammer,
everything he encounters begins to look like a nail.

— Abraham H. Maslow

Communication is measured less by what you say and more by what is heard. As a thought leader, it is your responsibility to communicate your message in a way that is understood. This is what IP Snapshots are for. Taking an IP Snapshot and spinning it out through all the different delivery methods or modes is the final piece in sharing your ideas with the world and making the difference you were born to make. (As you'll see we use method and mode interchangeably.)

This requires both flexibility and capability in equal doses. You need to develop a broad capability to communicate in any situation. You need to be able to then access those skills and adjust your delivery style as required — and select the right channel or delivery mode.

There are three broad personal communication channels. Knowing which part of your ideas to share, in which mode, is critical to ensuring how you get your message to your market.

As we mentioned earlier there are three broad delivery channels:

1. **Tell** — where you deliver great ideas through stories and examples.

2. **Show** — where you deliver great ideas through a learning process.

3. **Ask** — where you deliver by asking questions that lead people to your ideas.

There are six delivery modes altogether. We suggest you package your thought leadership so that it can be delivered across all or any of these six modes. Many people make the mistake of picking one mode to deliver their expertise through, and stick only to that. Speakers make money through speaking, trainers make money from training; coaches from coaching. And so on. Thought leaders need to stabilize their cash flow and grow revenue more quickly by diversifying how they deliver the information they provide. Remember, it is much easier to get $100,000 per year from each of the six modes that to get $600,000 per year from one.

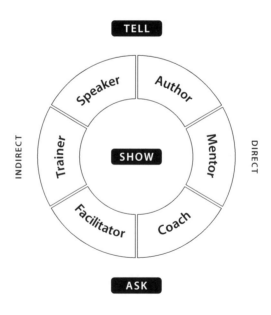

APPROACHES TO DELIVERING YOUR MESSAGE

We can give advice directly (one to one) or indirectly (one to many) through these three channels.

Direct

The direct modes allow you to focus immediately on the recipient as an individual. It is the communication that is intended to be sent with the individual in mind.

- Tell = Authorship

- Show = Mentor

- Ask = Coach

Indirect

The indirect modes allow you to deliver your message to a larger group. It is not so much targeted to an individual but more to a group of individuals.

- Tell = Speaker

- Show = Trainer

- Ask = Facilitator

In the *message* section you learned how to create an IP Snapshot of your ideas with three distinct yet aligned components: a content piece, a concept piece and a context piece. You use all three elements when you communicate, but one of these three takes priority depending on the channel or mode you are presenting through.

Looking at the focus of each channel:

- The tell channel is mainly about content.

- The show channel is mainly about concept.

- The ask channel is mainly about context.

SIX KEY CAPABILITIES TO THINK ABOUT IN EACH OF THE SIX MODES

What follows are six key capabilities to think about in each of the six modes. They are organized with one major and five minor skills that you need to develop. We have developed 102 specific skills and 102 commercial actions you need to consider across these modes. When we teach them, though, we do so in three layers, ensuring that thought leaders focus only on those skills for which they need to get their capabilities functional in each mode. Mastery is a great pursuit but often one achieved at some commercial cost. Speak well enough to share your ideas, coach well enough to serve your ideas but leave mastery for later. In other words, get on with it, then when you are up and running get good at it. The following pages are good to revisit when you are thinking about any of the channels.

Speaker mode

Speaking is about telling. It often involves speaking to many people in a direct way that delivers a specific message. Speaking is the broadcast channel. The minute a thought leader gets a large audience, they are able to influence significantly more people than in the other modes. It's a leveraged way to gain influence. The nature of the experience is such that people get caught up in the positive energy of the crowd as they respond to your great ideas. Speakership is the twenty-first century voice of leadership. It is the key to greater influence and engagement and to driving energy through your business.

KEY SPEAKING SKILL: *Message management*
A great speaker can organize gorgeous messages into a flowing narrative that the audience can swim through. From storytelling to making meaning, world-class presenters are masters of message.

SPEAKING SKILL 1: *Focus attention*
Great speakers are able to focus the attention of the audience. It's as if normal conversation becomes white noise. The speaker lines up their key ideas in a way that communicates absolute certainty, leaves very little open to interpretation and is unambiguous. Speakers are also able to focus attention through clever use of movement, gesture and language selection. In doing so, they can focus the attention of the audience.

SPEAKING SKILL 2: *Crystallize a point*
Due to their ability to organize their thinking and speaking around specific and discrete ideas, great speakers are able to deliver their message in a clearly defined package. When a thought leader speaks, the audience is left in no doubt as to what it was they said.

SPEAKING SKILL 3: *Establish relevance*
A thought leader is so confident in their message that they can afford to tailor their examples and customize the details of their ideas in a way that increases the relevance and meaning for everyone in the room.

SPEAKING SKILL 4: *Talk it up and down*
Great speakers use the power of abstraction to take any specific example or point they are making and tie it into some larger existential or metaphysical idea. In so doing, they are able to engage the global thinkers in the room: those who need to understand the big picture as well as those who need more concrete specific detail.

SPEAKING SKILL 5: *Inspire people to take action*

To be an awesome, rock star presenter, you have to change the human condition for those in the room. This means that, as a result of what you say and the power of your word, you inspire the audience to do something.

Motivation comes from within, no doubt, so the best you can hope to do is to breathe life into, and inspire, the people in the room. In our opinion, the measure of a successful presentation is the effect it has after the speech is over — the actions that people take as a result of what you've said.

Authorship mode

Like speaking, authorship is also about telling. It is the transference of your message to others in their time and in their place. Alongside speaking, writing is one of the most powerful and common means of delivering thought leadership. Writing enables you to speak with one voice to many people at great distances regardless of time and, if translated, even across many language barriers. Writing gives you huge leverage in a global market.

'Author' comes from the root word *authority,* and being an author immediately positions you as an authority in a chosen topic. Usually, when we think of a writer or author we automatically assume that they write books. This has been the traditional model for the past 400 years. However, during the past two decades, and especially in the past five years, authorship has reached the electronic age. Thought leaders now publish their ideas not only in books but also via white papers, e-zines, blogs and Twitter. In fact, in many respects these electronic forms of writing are more effective than publishing a book. Electronic publishing can be written and distributed quickly to capture a moment and market interest — and e-books now outsell physical books!

Authorship also includes video and audio content as well as the written word. So a CD series or an online video program are both examples of authoring content.

KEY AUTHORSHIP SKILL: *Ability to invest*

Writing takes time, energy and planning. If you don't have the clarity of thought or time, writing will prove difficult. So the key skill to ensure you write is to develop the ability to invest in the process. We choose the word 'invest' deliberately. You have to input time, energy and thought in order to create a desired output, such as a blog, article or book.

AUTHORSHIP SKILL 1: *Ability to focus and stay on track*

There are many ways of doing this and the trick is to find one that works for you. Matt, for example, writes on a computer that is completely dedicated to writing. There are no games, presentation files or emails available on this laptop to distract him. Matt constantly finds that while writing one book, including this one, he gets ideas for another. Hence to ensure he stays focused he keeps a trusty moleskin notebook next to him so that he can quickly capture his random thoughts and then return to the manuscript to continue writing.

AUTHORSHIP SKILL 2: *Maintain momentum*

Once you start writing, write regularly. There is a magic that occurs in writing when you get in the flow. Writing regularly tends to increase the frequency of writing in flow. Writing in flow, if you have never heard of or experienced it, feels as if you are simply taking dictation, as your thoughts or the universe or your genius provide the ideas and words, and your fingers write or type them.

AUTHORSHIP SKILL 3: *Work to a structure*

Thought leaders mostly write in the non-fiction genre. Non-fiction requires logical sequencing to support the reader's access to your thinking. Developing a structure to write with saves time, keeps your writing sequential and inevitably makes your writing easier to read and more easily understood and digested.

AUTHORSHIP SKILL 4: *Come from clarity*
Thought leadership is an exciting discipline and art. Once you begin to practice, ideas seem to flow in. Using your 'Pink Sheets' or IP is the best way to ensure you are creating and sequencing your thoughts from a position of clarity.

AUTHORSHIP SKILL 5: *Think both as the receiver and as the author*
It sounds obvious saying this, but many of a thought leader's readers will not have as much in-depth understanding of or experience with their subject as they do. It pays to write accordingly. Write so that even someone new to your topic can comfortably follow your thinking and absorb your ideas. It is so easy to fall into the trap of using jargon or technical language, or to even to assume that your reader already understands something about the concept you are writing about.

Training mode

Training is about showing. Often it is a sharing a process with a group of people that enables them to learn a new skill. Training allows you to show others what they need to do — and how to do it. It is about providing a set of skills and a process to create a behavioral change across a group of people. Many thought leaders will have used their genius to identify a new way to do things. Training allows others to take these ideas and implement them step-by-step in the pursuit of a better outcome. This is a skill, as it requires thought to analyze the unseen steps that occur in a particular way. It also forces you to find new ways of showing how to improve skills and capabilities.

When you develop an effective training approach and the groups are training enthusiastically and apply what you have taught them, great things happen. Targets are surpassed, people are unified, and results are amplified across a group of people who are aware that they have accomplished something that they might not have been able to before the training.

KEY TRAINING SKILL: *Establish process*
Training is all about the step-by-step process that is used to show what needs to be done. Great trainers establish a process that transfers learning and skills effectively.

TRAINING SKILL 1: *Drive content objectives*
Being clear on the outcomes you want your trainees to achieve is one of the keys to successful training. The most dynamic trainer in the world can be interesting and share lots of stories but completely miss the point. Training is only effective if those attending your training are able to implement the new skills and achieve a result.

TRAINING SKILL 2: *Review and refresh content creatively*
You need to ensure that you build into your training a way to repeat the key messages in numerous ways. This is critical given the different learning styles of individuals as well as the different experiences they bring into the training environment. People who have been in a role or organization for a period of time may have been introduced to what you are going to train them in, so it is important to refresh your content.

There's an old saying, tell 'em what you're going to say, say it, then tell 'em what you've said. And it's true — but you can't just say the same words three times. You need to have different ways to get the same message across.

TRAINING SKILL 3: *Engage interest*
Almost everyone has been to a boring training program where the trainer fails to grab the attention of the group. To fully open up someone to learning a new skill, you must engage them in a way that they want to be there and want to learn. The group dynamics of training allow for collective engagement. This is, however, dependent

on your ability to consistently engage the trainees and capture their ever-shortening attention spans.

TRAINING SKILL 4: *Design effective curriculum*
One critical area that separates training from the other modes is a specific agenda or curriculum that the trainer is going to follow in teaching others. This requires time to create the best framework for the skills that need to be taught. More than likely you will need to include the main point, the way that you will share this point with the group and the process that you will use to allow them to practice this new knowledge or skill.

TRAINING SKILL 5: *Vary teaching techniques*
By varying your training approach, you will increase your group's learning and ability. Training is more than standing at the front of a room and telling the trainees what the step-by-step process is. You need to be able to use a blend of training methods to embed the learning. This could include interactive discussions, real-time role plays, dyadic activities, case studies, partner interviews and a range of other techniques to help drive the learning into their minds — and their actions!

Mentoring mode

Mentoring is about sharing your past experience. This is often in a one-to-one setting allowing you to show insights that you gained in similar situations or similar roles. You actually get to participate in the journey of the person you mentor, and this helps refine your thinking and clarify your instincts in such a way that you can leverage them again and again. Rather than just getting the benefit, with mentoring you get to capture it.

This of course serves the person you mentor, but it serves you, the mentor, just as much. Mentors make it their job to understand what they do so well that they can reverse-engineer it for other people.

They have to go from being great at something to being masterful. The mastery comes when you know it inside and out and are able to teach the process to others so that they benefit.

KEY MENTORING SKILL: *Enhance experience*
Mentoring is all about experience. You cannot mentor someone in something in which you have no experience. It also needs to be experiential. The mentor creates experiences for the person they are mentoring.

MENTORING SKILL 1: *Expose personal experiences*
Your experiences need to be shared. We say 'exposed' because quite often the mentee will learn as much from your mistakes as from your successes. To be a great mentor you open your world to the mentee.

MENTORING SKILL 2: *Hold a threat-free space*
Of course, this applies to the person you are helping, but it also applies to you as the mentor. A mentee is normally ambitious enough to be robust and OK with whatever you dish out. They may even expect a bit of push from you. This skill is more about your ability to not feel threatened as they start to exceed expectations and really start to get some runs on the board.

MENTORING SKILL 3: *Allow for personal experiences*
You need to enjoy yourself as a mentor. Enjoy some personal experiences with the mentee — it is not all work. The benefit of experiencing you in more than one facet is key to the mentee's experience. Perhaps they come to your house for dinner or they sit with you and your kids one afternoon. It is a deeper, more holistic relationship than any of the other modes. Naturally, you need to manage your boundaries well with this. Just make sure it doesn't become 'friendtoring'!

MENTORING SKILL 4: *Make time in time*
Mentoring happens in both an informal and a formal structure. The formal structure might be a one-hour conversation every fortnight.

The informal structure might be picking you up from the airport or sharing a flight or attending a live meeting with you.

Great mentors make time in time — they fold their mentoring into other delivery. This enriches the experience of the mentee and is more efficient for the mentor.

MENTORING SKILL 5: *Personalize the learning*

Everything needs to be made relevant for the person being mentored. If you share a story of what once worked for you, you need to be sure to relate it to them and to whatever they are dealing with at the moment. Modern mentoring is a value exchange. For most of us it is a commercial offering (people pay to be mentored), which has forced us to do more than simply reminisce about our past wins and losses. Drive the relevance home.

Facilitation mode

Facilitating is about asking a group of people questions. Often this is to guide the group in a particular direction by drawing out their viewpoints. Facilitation allows you to draw out of a group of people their ideas, aspirations and thoughts. By asking questions of a group of people, you are able to set the tone of the discussion without telling them what ideas to discuss. This allows you to be viewed as a neutral guide encouraging exploration of issues, concerns or solutions that all come from the group. They have buy-in to the solutions because they feel that they helped to come up with them. Another advantage of facilitation is that it allows you to maximize your time by asking common questions of a group of people — rather than asking individually.

KEY FACILITATION SKILL: *Establish environment*

A great facilitator has the ability to create a trusting environment that will encourage their audience to fully participate. Without this supportive environment, true thoughts, viewpoints or ideas will not be aired.

FACILITATING SKILL 1: *Remove personal agenda*

You need to ensure that when you facilitate you remove your personal biases from the conversations. A group will quickly identify if you are trying to steer or control the discussion and this will limit your outcomes. It is important to leave your agenda behind — and focus on the themes that the group is sharing.

FACILITATING SKILL 2: *Create trust*

Without trust there is no honesty. Your role as a facilitator is to ensure that trust is built and encouraged. By establishing guidelines before the facilitation you can set the scene for this trust. However, during the discussion you will need to continue encouraging and recognizing honesty when shared.

FACILITATING SKILL 3: *Respect diversity*

You need to appreciate — and actually seek out — diversity of viewpoints and ideas when you facilitate. Often the individuals with opposing views add a new dimension to the same topic or idea. Some of the greatest innovations of our time have come from facilitated discussions that allowed for a broad range of views to be shared. Imagine where we would be if Apple had discounted the idea of the iPod when someone on their product team mentioned it in a discussion.

FACILITATING SKILL 4: *To not be attached to outcome*

True facilitation allows a process to be free flowing and move in numerous directions. You need to have a direction in mind, but not be tied to a specific outcome. By remaining detached from a particular end result you are able to focus on the group dynamics and quality of ideas being shared.

FACILITATING SKILL 5: *Active listening*

When facilitating it is your responsibility to ensure that every individual group member is heard. This requires an acute level of hearing because during a passionate discussion it is often the loudest individual that gets listened to. A thought leading facilitator has the unique ability to pick up on the quieter, yet just as valuable, comments that other group members make. Often this is a crucial turning point for a group, as these individuals have been processing the discussion and can provide extremely important insights — as long as they are heard.

Coaching mode

Coaching is about asking an individual key questions. Often it is about allowing them to explore their own viewpoints and reflect on the issues that they currently face. Coaching is the art of asking great questions of an individual in a one-on-one setting. To be a coach you do not need to be an expert in a particular skill, position or industry (unlike a mentor). You need to be able to ask powerful questions that inspire a higher level of thinking and understanding in your student. Coaching often provides a touch point that assists in focusing in on a particular area—without you having to tell them exactly what it is. Great coaches ask questions that plant a seed in the individual, which blossom to take their thinking to another level.

KEY COACHING SKILL: *Ensure agreement*

Coaching is all about the agreed relationship and result that aligns you and your student. You cannot coach someone in an area that they have no interest in. The coaching must be in an area that they agree to take on board — and implement!

COACHING SKILL 1: *Identify agenda*

You need to identify the agenda and the process that you will take in the coaching session. This is important as it allows you to paint a picture in the mind of your student of what will be discussed. Often the agenda will include: review of agreed tasks, current issues exploration and resetting of new tasks.

COACHING SKILL 2: *Check in regularly*
To make coaching powerful you need to continue it on a regular basis. Sitting down to ask questions and focusing on the individual is only part of the process. Coaching is about accountability and without follow-up check-ins over time the experience is limited. Commit to a series of coaching check-ins with the individual you are working with — they will often look forward to spending the time individually with you.

COACHING SKILL 3: *Assess deeper issues*
You need to be aware of the questions that you ask. Often they will start on the surface, but you will need to have a stable of questions that go deeper. These questions will often peel back the layers of understanding to reveal underlying sequences, themes or patterns that may need to be addressed.

COACHING SKILL 4: *Maintain perspective*
As a coach it is important to keep your perspective outside the individual and the issue. You need to allow them to fully understand the point you are making without telling them everything. Part of the brilliance in a coaching session is when the student comes to a new realization about something — without you as the coach directly telling them what it is.

COACHING SKILL 5: *Control overload*
One of the challenges that you may have as a coach is to try not to address too many areas in one session. Resist the temptation to identify ten issues for the individual to address, understand and implement. Have your student focus on three to five questions or specific areas before your next coaching session.

CHOOSE THE RIGHT MODE

Remember, you will need to select the most appropriate channel for the outcome that you desire. Be careful not to get 'stuck' by using just one delivery mode to get your message across. We will cover this in more detail in the next chapter. These skills take time and many thought leaders effortlessly demonstrate them naturally. Your task is to select the right channel for the right person at the right time. Also remember to refer back to these pages when you are deciding to create a cluster in a new mode. Reviewing these skills can help you to ensure that your delivery is worthy of a thought leader.

11.

Sequencing Your Channels

*You can never cross the ocean unless you have
the courage to lose sight of the shore*

— CHRISTOPHER COLUMBUS

One of the biggest questions that we get from people starting — or wanting to grow — their practice is: 'Which of the six modes should I start with?' There is no quick answer on this as it depends on a whole range of variables:

- What mode do you have capability in?

- What mode will the market prefer to buy?

- What mode can get you dollar productive the quickest?

If you have not developed a list, have no money and don't have an established IP, then offer a coaching cluster first. This is a safer mode to start in for a number of reasons. The first is that it allows you to co-create and further refine your IP. When working with an individual it also simplifies that communication to a one-to-one dynamic, which is more manageable than working with an audience. It also can mitigate the potential of negative consequences. If you make a mistake with an individual in a one-on-one coaching session, this is much more forgiving than if you are on stage delivering a speech to 250 people who disagree with your message and your delivery. Not to mention the damage to your reputation that may occur and hurt your future positioning!

One word of caution, there is not one definitive approach that you can take. It will be dependent on your expertise, skills and current abilities — and position in the marketplace if you have one already.

WHEN TO USE WHICH MODE

To be successful, you will need to select the most appropriate delivery method (mode) for the outcome that you, or more importantly your client, desire.

Be careful not to get 'stuck' by using just one delivery mode to get your message across. Also, never ever have your primary delivery mode on your business card. Every time we meet someone who has 'coach' or 'trainer' on their business card we cringe. This labels you — unfortunately — as being only able to deliver in just that one mode. You need to establish your expertise above the mode of delivery — and demonstrate that you have the capability to leverage your ideas in a range of delivery methods. Be a bespoke solution, not an off-the-rack one.

Remember these skills take time, and many masters demonstrate them naturally. Your task is to select the right channel for the right person at the right time! Developing mastery in the modes is key to sustaining a brilliant black-belt practice—which we will look at later. In this book we are focusing on the commercialization of the six modes and how we can use them to achieve strategic direction.

SELECTING THE FRUIT ON THE MONEY TREE

For those that have some experience in one of the delivery modes there is another alternative to consider. In the Thought Leaders community we often use a metaphor of a money tree to assist people in identifying where to start. Imagine that you have a tree that has fruit growing on it. The high-value fruit is positioned far above your head at the top of the money tree. The middle-value fruit is positioned in the middle of the money tree and the low hanging fruit is positioned at the bottom of the money tree within easy reach. How do you select which fruit to go for?

Be careful to not make the overly ambitious decision to go immediately for the high hanging fruit. An example of this is a coach who is currently charging $150 per hour deciding to become a speaker and charge $10,000 per hour. This is a very large jump and most people do not have the skills in the delivery modes to be able to go for this high hanging fruit — and they often do not have the positioning to charge the fees that can be charged at this level.

So given this situation, where is the easiest place to start? The low hanging fruit. It can be smarter to start with the delivery modes that you already have some skill and ability in. It may be that you simply did not have your message or cluster identified to allow you to commercialize your expertise properly. Or it could be that you did not package up or charge the fee that you are worth — or that may be in line with the current marketplace for someone with that expertise and positioning.

MONEY FOR JAM

There is one more level to the money tree. This is the fruit that has already ripened and often fallen off the tree and can be found on the ground. If you have ever been to an orchard you will have seen this fruit on the ground or over-ripened on the tree.

While lots of us make the mistake of just stepping over that rotting fruit, most farmers do not waste it — they gather it and turn it into jam. It is a process that has a few more steps and is not as nice as a fresh piece of fruit, however it can generate income nonetheless.

For some people the best progress will be made if they start with their jam opportunities before reaching up for the fresh fruit. These may be the clusters that you have been delivering for in the past that you are trying to move away from or are bored with. Or just the things that people are still asking you to do, but you think of as your past rather than the future.

For example, if you came out of a career in real estate, that's where your jam might be. In your mind you've moved on, it's not where you want to work anymore. However, that's where you have experience and networks, so it's worth finding a cluster there to start with. Perhaps coaching women in real estate, or training new agents, or facilitating monthly real estate team meetings. Not everything that you did previously, but something that is easy to make money from.

This may not be the sexiest place to start, however we call it 'making money for jam'. For many people it is important to gain momentum and take action. Once you get this momentum occurring, then you can begin expanding your focus in your 90-day projects that will involve new clusters and delivery modes.

RIGHT ANGLE PLANNING

To identify which delivery modes to add to your strategy we recommend what we call right angle planning. Placing an imaginary right angle over the model we can identify eight different combinations of three modes which require complementary skills.

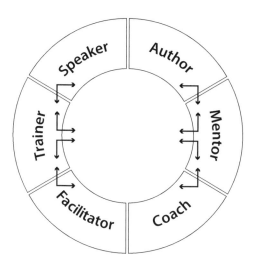

The eight combinations are:

- Speaker, Author, Mentor
- Trainer, Speaker, Author
- Trainer, Mentor, Author
- Trainer, Mentor, Coach

- Speaker, Trainer, Mentor
- Facilitator, Trainer, Mentor
- Trainer, Facilitator, Coach
- Facilitator, Coach, Mentor

So if, for example, you are primarily a facilitator, then you have three combinations of two additional modes available to you: Trainer and Coach; Trainer and Mentor; or Coach and Mentor. Facilitating requires similar skills to coaching — they are both 'ask' modes. Speaking and coaching on the other hand are quite different. Coaching is one on one, speaking is one to many. Coaching is 'ask', speaking is 'tell'. So its harder to jump from coaching to speaking.

From past experience we also know that most of our black belts deliver their clusters in the speaker-author-mentor (or SAM) modes. Often these modes allow for the positioning and charging of higher fees which can help you get to black belt easier. This is not to say that you cannot become a black belt using the trainer-facilitator-coach modes, because we have a number of people in our community who have. What we have noticed, however, is that these modes take much more effort and energy because the marketplace often has fee ceilings that limit the revenue in each of these modes. There are always exceptions to the rule, but this is what we have noticed after working with thousands of people.

Plan your delivery modes based on the right angles and improve your skills and abilities to increase your revenue.

CROSS PROMOTION OPPORTUNITIES

Depending on which modes you are delivering in, there are opportunities to cross promote into other modes. This is an excellent leverage strategy that can help you to increase your impact with an organization and increase the income across more than one delivery mode.

Speaker/author leads itself for an easy cross promotion to mentor. For example, after speaking at a conference, the CEO who was in the audience may come to you and ask if you could do one-on-one mentoring for themselves and their team. You have already impressed them with your message and your ability as an expert to deliver this message, and now they are asking you to provide that message using another delivery mode for their company. If you have authored a book that positions you further as an expert, it is also easier to be asked to deliver a mentoring offering.

If you are leading a facilitation session for a corporate retreat, you could be asked to develop a training program to teach their internal learning and development team to run your facilitation process. Once again this is a cross promotion opportunity that positions you as the thought leader in a particular area and allows you to have a much greater impact.

Not all modes are created equal:

- The *tell* modes (speaker and author) require you to have platforms and a list. A list of people will buy your book if you tell them about it. Equally, there is no point having a speech if you can't find a bunch of people in a room who are happy to let you stand on a platform and share your ideas. You've got to know *people*.

- The *show* modes (trainer and mentor) need you to have deep knowledge and contacts. If you don't know people who can help accelerate the career path, then it's hard to be a mentor. Equally, if you don't know a subject inside out, then it's hard to be a trainer of much worth. You've got to know *something*.

- The *ask* modes (facilitator and coach) require you to have deep relationship skills and to be tuned into what is happening for people in the moment. It's about an awareness of what's happening in you, in them, and in the room or conversation. You've got to *be present*.

TRANSACTIONAL AND LEVERAGED APPROACHES

Each of the six modes has both transactional and leveraged versions. Transactional approaches are the most common. They are the easiest to understand and sell, as the delivery is often captured by an individual unit or item. Typically this is based on a segment of time, such as the delivery of a training day or an individual coaching session. The transaction is that others pay you for the service you provide during that unit of time. This is a very common method when starting off, and many industries have commonly understood benchmark fees that a trainer, coach or speaker would get paid. This is where most people should start with their practice, as it allows you to build pieces of IP that you can combine and sell to others.

Once your practice is better established, a more leveraged model is achieved by blending a number of these modes into an overall package. This could involve a series of training events, or licensing your IP to a client that allows them to deliver it internally with their people. Generally, people will need to have created a range of IP areas and honed their skills in the various delivery formats. A word of caution: be careful not to over-promise and under-deliver these leveraged models before you have developed your IP fully and have had successful experience in delivery. Leverage is the focus of someone at the red-belt level, and thus requires the proper foundations in place to ensure success.

We have created the following table to allow you to see the different transactional and leveraged options across each of the six delivery modes.

Speaker

TRANSACTIONAL
Corporate speaker on professional conference circuit.

$5,000
per speech

LEVERAGED
Speak at networking events with a $5k success system in product or service offerings at back of room. Average 20 sales to audiences of 150.

$100,000
per speech

Author

TRANSACTIONAL
Sell self-published book at back of room and through your website. Sell 1,000 copies at $30 each.

$30,000
life of book

LEVERAGED
Build a membership website. Sell 100 annual memberships at $1000.

$100,000
per year

Trainer

TRANSACTIONAL

Trainer at $4,000 per training day.

$4,000
per day

LEVERAGED

License your IP to an organization. Train 6 internal trainers at $5,000 each, then charge per person for 250 members at $500 per head.

$125,000

Mentor

TRANSACTIONAL

Offer 10 private mentoring sessions at $500 per session.

$5,000
per client

LEVERAGED

Run quarterly group mentoring sessions (including some one-on-one sessions) at $12,000 per year. Sell to 30 people.

$360,000
per year

Facilitator

TRANSACTIONAL

Facilitation sessions at $4,000 per day. Get 3 days a year per client.

$12,000
per client

LEVERAGED

Run weekend residential retreats for $2,500 per head. Get 55 people to attend.

$137,500
per retreat

Coach

TRANSACTIONAL

Sell coaching sessions to individuals in organizations for $10,000 for 8–12 sessions.

$10,000
per client

LEVERAGED

Certify coaches in the use of your methodology for $12,000 plus $5,000 per year. Get 12 coaches.

$180,000
per year

The delivery modes also act as strategy filters. Each mode helps you organize your ideal cluster — and leverage your income. The more successful you become, the higher the skill, all leading toward the pursuit of mastery.

12.

Pursuit of Mastery

Mastery is great, but even that is not enough.
You need to be able to change course without
a bead of sweat, or remorse.

— TOM PETERS

To be a true thought leader there needs to be an obsessive desire to improve one's skills, approach and impact with others. Million dollar plus thought leaders practices typically have three mega clusters that each bring in $250,000 to $500,000 dollars each. To secure and maintain this, the thought leader must be masterful at each of the modes behind the clusters. If one cluster is to make money speaking on the conference circuit they must be a brilliant speaker, not just a good one.

But, don't be lured by mastery early on.

This is a mistake that many people make in the early days of building their thought leaders practice. It often happens when they get stuck commercially. For some, it's easier to enroll in a course to become a better coach than to go and have a meeting with someone who will either give you feedback or finance, both great currencies. Don't use mastery of method as a form of procrastination. Get started training, don't sign up for a course on 'how to train'.

If you are using your IP, as developed through your pink sheets, you don't need to be master of delivery yet. You are the author of the idea, as such we don't need you to be the best at sharing that idea initially. Just be good enough and get going.

KEY ACTIVITIES IN EACH OF THE MODES

In addition to the skills provided in the earlier chapters, we wanted to offer five Stage 1 actions to take in each delivery mode in order to get your revenue to $10,000 per month in that mode. We then suggest an additional five Stage 2 actions to take you from $10,000 to $20,000 per month, and five Stage 3 actions to take you beyond $20,000 per month. These are not the only activities that you could do. However, in working with people we have found that having a process to follow helps them to focus on doing more of the things they need to do to increase capability, and less of the things that are a distraction.

One thing to be aware of: the following section contains a vast range of information. Feel free to jump around and focus on the mode that you feel is your current strength or next opportunity.

Five key actions for speaking

The following actions are critical for getting you started in the speaking mode. They will help you establish the speaking component of your practice and build your first $10,000 in this mode.

SPEAKING ACTION 1: *Discover your big word*
This is more than the topic for your talk — it is the context that many different talks and clusters can fit under. Your big word is the lens through which all your thoughts are filtered. Thought Leaders Partner Gabrielle Dolan has 'authenticity' as her big word. If you want to transition your organization towards real talk, real communication, you'd get Gabrielle in. Equally, if you want your executive team to

understand the power of storytelling in business, Gabrielle's the one you'd call.

What's your big word? If you don't know, go with what you think it is. You can always change it down the track if you need to.

SPEAKING ACTION 2: *Write and rehearse a presentation*

Take your IP Snapshots and turn them into a speech. What are the 3–5 points you want to make, and what are the stories, case studies and examples you will use to back them up? Add an introduction and a close, and you have the beginnings of your presentation. Then it's time to rehearse. Give your presentation to a wall, to a photo of an audience, to your steering wheel when you are driving. Rehearse it until it's in your body, until you don't need your notes or your slides, and you could almost do it backwards.

SPEAKING ACTION 3: *Deliver it to an invited group and/or to service clubs*

There is only one way to get better at speaking, and that's to speak. Lots. So before you go to a speaking bureau or a conference organizer and ask for $5,000 to give your talk, deliver it to lower-risk audiences. Invite a bunch of people you know to come and hear it. Alternatively, service clubs are always looking for free speakers, so volunteer to deliver to a few.

SPEAKING ACTION 4: *Offer a low-investment preview or special-deal sessions to prospective clients*

Give your talk at a brown-bag lunch. Include it in a training package. Offer it as a preview before a company conference so they can test it before rolling it out before the whole company. Cut whatever deals you need to in order to get it in front of people.

SPEAKING ACTION 5: *Collect testimonials*

As you are delivering your talk to all these different audiences, make sure you are collecting testimonials. Ask people what they loved about your talk, and what is going to change in their lives as a result of what you said. It's even more powerful if you can gather testimonials saying what actually changed, but you can't generally get those at the time so that takes a bit more organization. Get into the habit of handing out testimonial forms when you give your presentation. Craig Rispin, another Thought Leaders Mentor, is the master at this — he collects his testimonials on LinkedIn, and has more than 400.

Additional speaking actions

Once you have taken the five foundational actions, and have achieved revenue of $10,000 per month in your practice, the following Stage 2 actions will help you get from $10,000 to $20,000 a month, and the Stage 3 actions will take you beyond $20,000.

STAGE 2 SPEAKING ACTIONS — *$10,000 to $20,000*

- Write a 100-word summary of the presentation.

- Outline 2–5 key topic benefits as bullet points.

- Create a 150-word bio on why you are the expert on the topic.

- Approach network gatherings/business breakfasts and offer to speak.

- Write a 1,500-word article around the 'problems, causes and solutions' that the presentation addresses, and send it to the groups in your network.

STAGE 3 SPEAKING ACTIONS — *$20,000+*

- Create a fee schedule.

- Advertise the presentation to key people.

- Create an admin pack that sets up expectations once confirmed to speak.

- Scope up the book of the speech.

- Embed sales and positioning into your presentation.

Five key actions for authoring

The following actions are critical for getting you started in the authoring mode, and will help you to establish the authoring component of your practice and build your first $10,000 in this mode.

AUTHORING ACTION 1: *Pick a topic and do a thorough literature review*

Imagine you are doing a PhD on your topic — that's the sort of literature review you want to do. You need to be on top of all the significant books and journal articles in your area, and read these as a thought leader. Have two pads beside you as you read; keep one list of points that you can add to, and one of points that you disagree with. You want to be adding to the field, not just regurgitating it.

AUTHORING ACTION 2: *Scope out your message uniqueness*
Your literature review will help you know what the current thinking is, and how your message is unique. To be a thought leader and to develop original thinking that people will pay a premium for — your message needs to be unique.

AUTHORING ACTION 3: *Come up with six titles and bylines*
These will come from the middle section of your IP Snapshots. You want to make the titles catchy and the bylines explanatory — each of these should be of the caliber where you could create a book with that title and byline.

AUTHORING ACTION 4: *Write 1,000–1,500 words on one title*
Do this with a view to selling them to print media. The aim of this is not so much for the revenue as for the positioning, and the process

of doing the writing. Having your articles published in print media adds credibility and makes you an expert in your area.

AUTHORING ACTION 5: *Record an interview on each topic and sell it to your network*

This can be either with you as the interviewee, or you interviewing other experts in your area. It is equally great positioning for you to be bringing experts in your field together under your banner, so don't shy away from doing this just because you're not the one speaking the IP. An interview series in either direction can position you as an expert.

Additional authorship actions

Once you have taken the five foundational actions, and have achieved revenue of $10,000 per month in your practice, the following Stage 2 actions will help you get from $10,000 to $20,000 a month, and the Stage 3 actions will take you to beyond $20,000.

STAGE 2 AUTHORING ACTIONS *— $10,000 to $20,000*

- Create a table of contents for your book and scope out relevant IP Snapshots.

- Write the front and back cover and get feedback on angle/content.

- Create and sell a column to print and/or electronic media.

- Design a $1,000 product-offering around your topic, and market it to your network.

- Decide on your production model and create a project schedule, including critical stages.

STAGE 3 AUTHORING ACTIONS — *$20,000+*

- Allocate funds and timetable your book project.

- Recruit and brief a production team.

- Record and transcribe everything you do.

- Complete your first book.

- Leverage one product into many.

Five key actions for training

The following actions are critical for getting you started in the training mode and will help you establish the training component of your practice and build your first $10,000 per month in this mode.

TRAINING ACTION 1: *Review 'solutions audit' for market/message*
Conduct a market survey, then select the appropriate IP. Survey your target market about the biggest challenges they are facing, what is keeping them awake at night and what problems they need solving. Then select your IP that meets this challenge. Offer to give the results of the study back to the participants as a special report. This is great research, but it is also a great marketing move.

TRAINING ACTION 2: *Write a 300-word report/module on each component of the audit*
Next, integrate IP from your IP Snapshots and develop all modules into a 'mega-proposal'. This is an example of authority selling which is discussed in the 'Your market' section. You are creating a proposal before you have diagnosed problems for an individual client. In effect, you are saying to prospects: 'In your industry these are the major problems. If you are experiencing these problems, I can help.'

TRAINING ACTION 3: *Interview a target and test the applicability of the report*

Meet with a prospect, and go over the report results that are part of your proposal. Make sure that it lands — that it hits the right buttons — and that you will be able to sell training to address the problems identified.

TRAINING ACTION 4: *Design a mini training program and price it up*

As well as identifying which IP you will use for your training program, you need a price. If you are doing a public-channel training program, your price will generally be per person. If it is in the professional channel, it will typically be an overall price. So a two-day public workshop about personal finance might cost $990 per person. A one-day professional workshop about innovation might cost $7,500 total.

TRAINING ACTION 5: *Run a pilot program*

Create a lesson plan using IP Snapshots and modules. Once you have done that, run a pilot version and ask for testimonials/referrals. A pilot program is a great way to get started. It means you can reduce the cost without damaging your brand, and if one or two pieces don't really land it doesn't matter as much. Make sure you get lots of testimonials, and ask for referrals.

Additional training actions

Once you have taken the five foundational actions, and have achieved revenue of $10,000 per month in your practice, the following Stage 2 actions will help you get from $10,000 to $20,000 a month, and the Stage 3 actions will take you beyond $20,000.

STAGE 2 TRAINING ACTIONS — *$10,000 to $20,000*

- Write a simple 'white paper' (500–1,000 words) outlining the results that can be expected from the program, and distribute to referrals and your network.

- Create a learning program that incorporates all the various learning channels.

- Document the process in a facilitators' guide.

- Convert pilots and referrals to paid programs.

- Write a 1,500-word article around the 'problems, causes and solutions' that the program addresses, and distribute to participants as follow-up.

STAGE 3 TRAINING ACTIONS — *$20,000+*

- Send the article to your network and referrals.

- Create an admin pack that sets up expectations once confirmed to train.

- Develop sub-trainers.

- Appoint master trainers.

- Write a keynote address on the hottest, most unique component of the training program.

Five key actions for mentoring

The following actions are critical for getting you started in the mentoring mode, and will help you establish the mentoring component of your practice and build your first $10,000 per month in this mode.

MENTORING ACTION 1: *Evaluate your experience*

Determine whether you have experience that could help others, and specifically define *who* could benefit. Mentors are people who have 'been there, done that.' Coaches don't necessarily need the same experience. If you have never been a CEO involved in a merger, you are not in a position to mentor CEOs about successfully managing mergers (although you may be able to coach them). A good indicator that you are ready to mentor in a particular area is when you have lots of people offering to buy you a coffee and pick your brain. Start buying your own coffee, and sell them a mentoring program instead!

MENTORING ACTION 2: *Find ten people to help promote your mentoring*

Identify ten people who have already asked you to share your experience, and ask them for testimonials/referrals. These are the people who have bought you coffee in the past and picked your brains. Again, you can't have too many testimonials.

MENTORING ACTION 3: *Write a one-page background piece*

Write on what you have done and how others can benefit from sharing your experience. This is your biography tailored to the mentoring program you are offering. If you are looking to mentor CEOs on managing mergers, write about when you were a CEO during a merger and how successful it was, and about all the other CEOs you have helped go through mergers. If you don't have a good design aesthetic yourself, get a designer to brand this and include your photo. It should look good — you want this to be forwarded on to other people.

MENTORING ACTION 4: *Contact the ten referrers and send them the background piece*

The aim here is not just to impress the ten referrers, but to have them forward this to other people they know. By making it easy for your referrers — as you have written the background piece — they're more likely to spread your name and make introductions on your behalf.

MENTORING ACTION 5: *Invite them to meet with you*

Offer to meet the people you have been introduced to through your referrers, one-on-one. Schedule the meetings over two days and ask them questions around your sales model. Follow up the background piece with an invitation to meet for coffee (this time *you* are buying the coffee!) The aim of the meeting is primarily to provide value and then to sell a mentoring program if appropriate. Ask them questions about the problems they are experiencing, share a bit of your IP to give them some value, and if they are someone you would like to work with, invite them to participate in a mentoring program.

Additional mentoring actions

Once you have taken the five foundational actions, and have achieved revenue of $10,000 per month in your practice, the following Stage 2 actions will help you get from $10,000 to $20,000 a month, and the Stage 3 actions will take you beyond $20,000.

STAGE 2 MENTORING ACTIONS — *$10,000 to $20,000*

Create a special report that demonstrates your wisdom on the topic.

- Design a monthly retainer program and flyer.

- Invite the initial ten prospects to join
  your mentoring program.

- Meet this core group monthly, bed down
  the process and ask for referrals.

- Create a lead-generation process on the topic.

STAGE 3 MENTORING ACTIONS — *$20,000+*

- Submit articles to industry journals and magazines.

- Consider ways to group mentees for leverage
  (once retainer and process is established).

- Interview successful mentees and discuss results/outcomes.

- Collect written testimonials.

- Create a marketing piece, and mail to target audience.

Five key actions for facilitating

The following actions are critical for getting you started in the facilitation mode, and will help you establish the facilitation component of your practice and build your first $10,000 per month in this mode.

FACILITATION ACTION 1: *Scope out 6–12 situations where your message applies*

The example we used earlier — Gabrielle Dolan's message on authenticity — could apply in a number of different situations. It could apply to a sales team looking to increase their numbers. It could also apply to the senior leadership team of an organization that has plateaued. Equally, it could apply to a start-up business conducting a strategic planning exercise. Which situations would your message apply to?

FACILITATION ACTION 2: *Design a loose process that works over 1, 2 or 3 days*

The process needs to work for the situations where you have identified that your message applies. Remember that facilitating requires you to ask questions and manage the context. Most of the content comes from the group. However, thought leadership facilitation is different from pure facilitation — your aim is not to be invisible. You use your IP to bring everything together, and to make meaning of the content you have drawn out of the group.

FACILITATION ACTION 3: *Prepare with the appropriate IP beforehand*

Great facilitation looks like magic. You listen all day, and then you create a model that ties everything together beautifully and provides the big picture for everything to fit inside. When your model is thorough, elegant and unique, you look like a genius. It actually comes from preparation. You identify the relevant IP beforehand, so that you go in armed with your points, models and metaphors. You elicit the content that fits your IP and then reveal your model at the end as you tie it all together.

FACILITATION ACTION 4: *Review 20 questions that your process solves, and select key ones*

Once you have created your facilitation process IP, identify 20 questions that lead towards your models. Identify the key ones that you will ask, and that will create useful content for your participants. For example, if you had some leadership IP around how vision, mission, core values and measurable results fit together, you would ask questions and facilitate sessions about each of these. Then at the end you would say, 'We have been talking about … and this is how it all comes together.'

FACILITATION ACTION 5: *Run a low-cost/pilot program for a target*

Deliver your facilitated process for a pilot group. After completion, write a report suggesting follow-up actions. The pilot program will get you your testimonials and your first case study, and the report may lead to ongoing coaching or mentoring work.

Additional facilitation actions

Once you have taken the five foundational actions, and have achieved revenue of $10,000 per month in your practice, the following Stage 2 actions will help you get from $10,000 to $20,000 a month, and the Stage 3 actions will take you beyond $20,000.

STAGE 2 FACILITATION ACTIONS — *$10,000 to $20,000*

- Design an ongoing version of the program with a monthly commitment.

- Suggest other programs that are designed for clients' situations.

- Create a follow-up process for action plans.

- Write a 1,500-word article around the 'problems, causes and solutions' that the program addresses, and send it to your entire network.

- Create a lead generation process on the topic.

STAGE 3 FACILITATION ACTIONS — *$20,000+*

- Interview prospects using 'solutions audit.'

- Convert pilots to full programs.

- Provide consultative support for the outcomes.

- Train sub-facilitators.

- Create a diagnostic tool.

Five key actions for coaching

The following actions are critical for getting you started in the coaching mode, and will help you establish the coaching component of your practice and build your first $10,000 per month in this mode.

COACHING ACTION 1: *Identify 20 people that you could coach*
Pick a category of individuals that you want to support, and a list of 20 people who match this category. The narrower your category is the more successful you will be (as discussed in the marketing chapter).

The more you know about these people the better, and ideally you have 20 of them already in your database.

COACHING ACTION 2: *Select 12 IP Snapshots that meet their needs*
Review '20 questions' for each of the 12 IP Snapshot and select key ones for sessions. Each coaching session will be based on one IP Snapshot, and you need to create 20 questions you could ask based on your IP. In pure coaching, you would follow where the individual is leading — this is not the case in thought leadership coaching.

COACHING ACTION 3: *Create a package of coaching sessions and scope the offering*
Your 12 IP Snapshots make up your coaching program. Work out what order makes sense, as some ideas may build on others. Next, map what the benefits of the whole program are to your target market. Then price the offering.

COACHING ACTION 4: *Invite the 20 people you identified to meet with you, one-on-one*
In the meeting, ask each person questions around your sales model. As with mentoring, your intention is to provide value during the session and then to sell a coaching program where appropriate.

COACHING ACTION 5: *Invite them to join your coaching program*
Make sure you don't finish the session without asking your prospect if they would like a coaching program. If they say yes, fill out a registration form on the spot, and schedule your first session.

Additional coaching actions

Once you have taken the five foundational actions, and have achieved revenue of $10,000 per month in your practice, the following Stage 2 actions will help you get from $10,000 to $20,000 a month, and the Stage 3 actions will take you beyond $20,000.

STAGE 2 COACHING ACTIONS — *$10,000 to $20,000*

- Over-service this first group by providing more than what is expected, and ask for referrals.

- Create a group-coaching version of your program.

- Offer to run an internal group session for one of your individual client's companies.

- Interview successful versions of your target clients.

- Create a lead-generation process on the topic.

STAGE 3 COACHING ACTIONS — *$20,000+*

- Publish the interviews from your coaching sessions in a book, CD, podcasts or newsletters.

- Create ongoing support groups for your clients.

- Write expertise positioning pieces on the messages.

- Create a selling/positioning presentation that identifies you as the expert coaching in your specialist area.

- Offer the presentation to target groups.

A LIFETIME JOURNEY

All of the above activities can help you get started in your journey. Just remember, the pursuit of mastery is a lifelong activity. Someone that has mastered a skill or approach has reached a higher level of ability that others often admire. If you have ever watched a master at work, their approach appears effortless and easy. In his book *Mastery*, best-selling author Robert Greene describes how someone who has mastered a particular skill has followed a particular journey in acquiring this skill. Greene studied great masters in history such as Leonardo da Vinci, Albert Einstein and Buckminster Fuller as well as modern day masters across a range of fields including neuroscience, robotic engineering and fighter pilots. What he found is that mastery is not the result of genetics or privilege, but of the effort and process. Mindset was vitally important to achieving mastery.

In the Thought Leader community we have also noticed a direct correlation. As people achieve higher levels of revenue they almost always have further developed their delivery abilities. Often in reaching black belt they have achieved a level of mastery in a particular mode. They have evolved to a higher level of understanding and ability. This is because they have put in the time, energy, effort and focus required to provide them with a healthy dose of resilience and insight that others may lack. All of them started with a number of smaller activities that allowed them to achieve these results. Remember to do the work — there are no shortcuts to mastery.

Steps to Success

13.

The Revenue
Ladder

When I dare to be powerful, to use my strength
in the service of my vision, then it becomes
less and less important whether I am afraid.

— AUDRE LORDE

In traditional Japanese martial arts (karate, judo, jiu-jitsu, kendo, aikido), there were originally only two belts — a white belt and a black belt. For years you wore a white belt, and then eventually you got your black belt. Typically it would take seven to ten years to get a black belt. Some schools and some styles still operate in this way. In the early 19th century, one of the judo masters decided to begin using multiple colored belts to help students identify their progress through their journey. It has since been adopted in many other forms of martial arts and is widely used today.

The purpose was to create a more efficient and effective training model based on gaining proficiency in certain techniques at each level before moving on to the next one. At white-belt level the student would practice and become proficient at the most basic techniques — a straight punch or a simple throw. At the higher levels, more complex moves would be introduced and the student would have a sense of their progress towards their goal of a black belt.

This process allows people to walk before they run. It also creates a trusted framework for focus: focus on this now, and you will then be able to focus on harder things later as you move up the belt 'ladder'. In martial arts there is always someone who comes along and wants to perform advanced moves on day one. Sometimes they pull it off. More often than not, though, they hurt themselves (which can create great learning) or hurt others (which is not so great). Even aside from a strong negative consequence, usually the result of skipping ahead to complex physical skills simply means failure. By their very definition, skills need to be built up piece by piece.

We see new players to the thought leaders game who try to sell their thoughts using advanced moves. Some pull it off, but most just hurt themselves and others.

THE THOUGHT LEADERS REVENUE LADDER

In the previously mentioned revenue ladder, we borrow the martial arts belts to identify the different stages, and to identify what to focus on at each stage.

Like learning a martial art, you will progress more quickly in your practice if you take the appropriate actions at the right time. This methodology tells you what to focus on and what to do at each level in order to move through the belts to black belt and beyond as efficiently and as painlessly as possible. The journey to black belt and beyond typically takes three years.

BELT	INCOME	FOCUS
5th Dan	$1,200,000	Distribution
4th Dan	$1,080,000	Capacity
3rd Dan	$960,000	Productivity
2nd Dan	$840,000	Engagement
Black Belt	$720,000	Investment
Red Belt	$600,000	Leverage
Blue Belt	$480,000	Positioning
Green Belt	$360,000	Activity
Yellow Belt	$240,000	Value
White Belt	$120,000	Decision

THE COMMON PITFALLS

In our experience in working with thousands of thought leaders building their million-dollar practices, we have identified a number of pitfalls that commonly occur when people are trying to climb these levels.

Failing to clarify your message and your market

We know of numerous individuals who were inspired to be their own boss and do their own thing, but did not have a message. Without a clear message around your thought leadership, it is hard for anyone to see what you offer that is different from everyone else.

Having a message that is not appealing to a specific market is also a common pitfall. We often see this with thought leaders who are trying to help everyone (and consequently end up helping no one). A life coach whose message is *live a fulfilling life* without targeting a specific client base will struggle to attract prospects. By clarifying your message and your market, you can avoid this pitfall.

Attempting to move up the revenue ladder too quickly

In many societies today, it appears that everyone is in a hurry. They are in a hurry to get to work, to make something happen, and to earn a million dollars a year. There are also a lot of 'get rich quick' schemes that promise to make you a pile of money in 6–12 months. We are always cautious about how quickly you move up the revenue ladder. Our philosophy is more of a 'get rich slow' plan that allows you to leverage your thought leadership into the direction you want as you gradually increase your income. Likewise, some 'infopreneurs' who have seen others reach the peak of success will try to mimic them — without having the foundations in place to move to the next level. Be wary of moving too quickly!

Over-investing in office, staff and overheads

We know of many people who left a very lucrative corporate career believing that they could step out of their office and suddenly become a successful consultant, only to crash and burn. Many of them spent hundreds of thousands of dollars of their hard-earned money to create the best city office with all the expensive office fit-outs and expenses — recreating the corporate environment they had become used to. Many of them found after 6–12 months that their cash reserves had disappeared and they did not know how they were going to pay for the next two-year office lease and keep the doors open. They had applied a typical established business model to a practice that they were creating. Be aware that creating a thought leader practice from scratch requires you to be everything and do everything. As we'll see in coming chapters, as you move up the revenue ladder you will eventually have a team to take over some of these tasks, but to start with, it's all you.

Doubting your ability to generate a black belt practice

Another big obstacle for many people is the inability to envisage themselves earning black belt income ($720k a year) as an expert running a thought leader practice. The voice in the back of your head will have plenty to say about it. *'Me, a black belt, who am I kidding? Yeah, maybe ... maybe some other people could do that, but who is going to pay that much money for what I have to say?'* Everyone, including the many black-belt experts that we interviewed, has had to deal with those voices and that doubt. However, once you make the decision and focus on the goal, rather than on the obstacles, these voices and doubts will start to disappear.

THE JOURNEY

This journey is an effective, tested and proven methodology for building a thought leadership practice efficiently, and funding the growth from cash flow. At the time of writing, there are hundreds of people that we know of who have focused on building black-belt practices following this methodology — you'll hear from some of them in the coming pages.

The journey from white belt to black belt typically takes three years, so you can anticipate climbing two belts a year. This is to say, if you are currently a white belt, aim to be a green belt in 12 months' time. If you are ambitious, by all means go faster than this — it has been done within a year.

Read the following chapters and focus on the five activities at your level as a minimum. If you have more time and more money, then certainly do some others. We suggest that you do them one rung above and one rung below where you are. A green belt would focus on the green-belt activities, plus the five for the yellow belt (below) and the five for the blue belt (above). So at any one time you have 15 key activities — enough to keep you very busy, but not so many as to be completely overwhelming.

14.

White Belt

Whether you think you can or
you think you can't, you're usually right.

— HENRY FORD

White belt is the first level on the Thought Leaders Revenue Ladder
— it's where your thought leaders practice is generating an income of
$10,000 a month, or $120,000 a year.

BELT	INCOME	FOCUS
5th Dan	$1,200,000	Distribution
4th Dan	$1,080,000	Capacity
3rd Dan	$960,000	Productivity
2nd Dan	$840,000	Engagement
Black Belt	$720,000	Investment
Red Belt	$600,000	Leverage
Blue Belt	$480,000	Positioning
Green Belt	$360,000	Activity
Yellow Belt	$240,000	Value
White Belt	**$120,000**	**Decision**

And while it's only the first level, getting to white belt is nothing to sneeze at given that the median income in Australia, New Zealand and the USA (as well as the rest of the world) is less than this amount. According to the International Coaching Federation's 2012 Global Coaching Survey, the average income for a coach globally is US$47,900. Based on this figure, it would be safe to say that most coaches do not even reach white belt. So, if you are at white belt, give yourself a pat on the back. You are already more commercially successful than most. And if you are still on your way to white belt, don't be disheartened by the numbers we're talking about — be inspired! Then get back to work and get to white belt.

FOCUS: DECISION

The focus at white-belt level is *decision*. The first decision at white belt is deciding to build a thought leadership practice. Are you playing this game? Do you have something worth saying? Are you prepared to extend the thinking in your field? Do you want to commercialize your thinking and deliver it through the six modes of speaker, author, trainer, mentor, facilitator and coach? Are you prepared to have your name up in lights? Are you inspired by the idea of getting paid extremely well to do work you love, with people you like, the way you want? Do you have the patience for a get-rich-slow scheme? Do you have the stamina and the resilience to put in the hard yards required to get there?

Making this decision requires a dedicated commitment to focus in on the area of expertise that you want to be known for. For many on this journey it also requires the ability to leave some things behind. The word 'decide' comes from the same family of words as homicide, suicide, regicide, and genocide. The suffix 'cide' has the root meaning 'to kill'. 'Decide' literally means to kill off the alternatives. It sounds a bit dramatic, but when we are starting out it is critical to realize this.

As a thought leader there are infinite possibilities for your practice. There are an infinite number of messages you could come up with and almost as many markets you could deliver your message into. You need to decide which message and which market, and kill off the others. Don't worry, we will come back to these others later, it's just not the time for it now. In fact, adding more back into the mix is a critical part of the strategy at later belts.

We have met many clever people who want to grow their practice, only to make the mistake of not narrowing their activity and thus not being able to maintain focus in the right direction. It's one of the challenges of being clever and competent. There are many different things that you could do and be successful at. However, it's not commercially smart to do them all, especially at white belt.

Starting to move up the Thought Leaders Revenue Ladder is a case of less rather than more. It takes discipline to focus on improving a handful of techniques that you begin to master — before you try to do everything else! Someone with a black belt in a martial art has lots of techniques at their disposal, from a straight punch to a flying back-kick. However, someone starting their martial arts journey as a white belt will focus on push-ups, sit-ups, and learning a straight punch over and over until they have it nailed. Only then will they look at moving up to the next level and introducing the next technique.

It's the same with your practice when you are beginning as a white belt. Resist the temptation to do too many 'higher-level' activities — activities that are often built on the critical foundations you establish at the lower levels. As a white belt, if you attempt these activities you may hurt yourself and your practice. Decide on one market, one message, and deliver that message to that market. We'll say more on how to do that shortly.

One decision we invite you to make is; 'I am going to be a black belt.' In Australia when people study a martial art such as aikido or karate, on average only 1 in 200 people make it to black belt. Often the reason is that they do not make the decision at the beginning to get to black belt, and therefore don't commit to the activity and discipline that it will take to achieve this level.

FIVE THINGS TO DO AT WHITE BELT

1. Commit to black belt

When we review the thousands of people who have attended or come into contact with the principles from the different Thought Leaders programs, we notice that many of them have never achieved white belt: $120,000 income per year. A big question to ask is 'Why not?' We believe that often they did not make the commitment to growing their practice. There are numerous reasons why this may occur, from not believing that they are capable or have much to offer, to having no real message, or maybe not having the entrepreneur mindset required to 'go it alone'. The first thing to do is to commit to making this happen.

With apologies to any vegetarians, there is a saying about bacon and eggs that captures this perfectly. The chicken is interested; the pig is committed. In his keynote address *Blood in the Water*, Adrian Rainey says: "Committed people make a decision to be mentally tough and to do the work. They have a clear picture of what they want and why they want it but they are open to how they get it. Instead of limiting themselves to the past or being slow to adjust their approach, they learn, change and dig deep to achieve the results they want. Committed people do whatever it takes."

At white belt, you need to make the decision to be a black belt, not just to make it to yellow belt. If you want to be elite at anything, you need to commit to taking all the steps, not just the first ones. A tennis player hoping to become elite doesn't merely commit to learning a good forehand. They commit to doing everything they need do to be elite — every piece of footwork, thousands of hours practicing serves, and endless strength and conditioning. So too must you commit to the whole journey to black belt.

In Thought Leaders Business School, there's a meme of #WWABBD — What Would A Black Belt Do? It's a great question to ask, and it helps everyone assume the mindset of a black belt before they get there.

2. Choose your message, market and method

The goal at white belt is to start making $10,000 a month from one *cluster* of *message, market* and *method*. Once you achieve this, then you add another cluster of message, market and method to get to $20,000 a month. This leads to building your practice one cluster at a time towards black belt. It is also critical that your clusters have sustainable revenue. It is of limited value to your practice if you run a workshop once and make $20,000 but then never run it again.

To get to white belt, you need to choose your first cluster: your first combination of message, market and method. This is counter-intuitive. If there are lots of things you can do for lots of different people, it seems like it would work better to promote all of it, to cast the net wide. But this doesn't work better. It diffuses your energy, and at white-belt level it makes you less attractive to all your markets. Be very attractive to just one market.

Pick one message and deliver that message to one market. In choosing your cluster, think about what you know and whose problems that solves. People will pay to have their problems solved. A common mistake going to market with a message is making it about what you want to say, not what problem you can solve for your target market (hopefully, problems that are keeping them awake at night). Someone might have a breadth of knowledge and passion in a particular area, but if this is not being communicated in a way that resonates with their target market, they won't have success selling it.

Take someone who wanted to position themselves as the thought leader of 'positive attitude'. Although this might be the message you are delivering, it is not the message to go to market with. No one is lying awake at night worrying about their positive attitude. They are worrying about how they can get the results that they want, or possibly how to influence those people who will contribute to their success. Depending on the target market, the message might be how to get better results, to get more sales, to have more influence, to be a more effective leader, to be a better parent, to get more dates. How to do all those things could come down to attitude, but don't lead with 'positive-attitude training' in your message to your market.

When you choose your market, pick a market you know. If you have never been the CEO of a large organization and don't know any of those CEOs, they are not your market. Pick a market you have some connection with. This takes the nervous energy out of approaching them and having conversations around how you can help them. An ignorance of market is not only commercially questionable, it's also a bit arrogant.

For your method, you can pick one or more of the delivery modes that were previously identified. We recommend starting simple, and selecting a delivery mode that you are comfortable with. For example, if you have experience as a trainer, then focus on that delivery method. If you don't have a database of potential contacts, then start with coaching. Coach is often the easiest to activate, as each person you meet is a potential client.

Make your niche as narrow as possible. Again this seems counterintuitive, but it's necessary and it works. A business coach who specializes in helping real-estate agents who are turning over between $500,000 and $1 million will be more successful than a business coach who works with any small business. Most white belts make the mistake of making their offering too broad.

3. Enhance your contact base

Having a valuable contact base which you are able to leverage well is one of the most powerful strategies you can implement early on in your practice. It will ensure ongoing touchpoints with your client base and help achieve revenue stability. These days, contact bases are managed by CRMs (Contact Management Systems). CRMs track your conversations and who is a prospect for which of your offerings, and also allows you to communicate effectively, efficiently and strategically with your people.

In each of your clusters you want to have a group of at least 150 people in your CRM who know you and value what you do. That's really important — in Australia you can buy a list of two million businesses who don't know you or value what you do for $300. And that is virtually useless to your practice. But 150 people who know you and value what you do is gold. Those people can give you your $10,000 a month and more. The plan set forth in this book is about relationships, not about spamming thousands of people hoping something will stick.

All CRMs will enable you to track and communicate with these people, and many will allow you to do a lot more than that, including but not limited to emails, newsletters, groups and more. There are numerous different CRMs that you can use which are local (installed and run from your computer, without needing a persistent internet connection) and many more in the cloud (you access via a browser and can easily access from anywhere in the world on any computer, and is usually the better way to go). From most simple and easy to use, to complex and feature heavy would be: Contactually, Pipedrive, Solve360, Insightly, ACT, Sales Force and InfusionSoft. We would recommend the more simple CRMs, as the large ones often have feature sets that are complex and cumbersome.

A good target to start with is to meet 150 people, let them know what you do and invite them to sign up for your electronic newsletter, and begin adding insights on a weekly or fortnightly basis. Once they sign up, add them to your CRM and start communicating with them regularly via your electronic newsletter and/or blog. While some CRMs can manage your emails/newsletters and do this for you, there are many specialized Email Marketing services which will integrate into the various CRMs.

We often suggest using Mailchimp to distribute our electronic newsletters, for three reasons:

1. It allows you to track the analytics — who opened what section.

2. It allows you to distribute through other social networks for greater leverage.

3. It's free for the first 2,000 email addresses that you send your newsletter to.

Managing your CRM is one of the most important activities to begin when you are starting your practice. Those who have skipped this step have had to deal with the challenge of inconsistent marketing touchpoints with their prospects — these are the people losing momentum and getting 'stuck' at white belt.

4. Hire your first virtual assistant

At the moment you're probably doing most of the administrative work yourself. Considering your day rate, this is an incredibly expensive option! Not to mention the fact that it's taking time away from your thinking, selling, and delivering.

At white belt, we recommend getting a full-time off-shore virtual assistant, a 'Gun VA'. What is a Gun VA, exactly? 'Gun' is an Australian colloquial term to describe anyone who is excellent and formidable with regards to some activity. A Gun VA is an invaluable partner who supports you in running your practice or business, at a fraction of the cost of hiring locally.

There are three stages to hiring a Gun VA — preparation, recruitment, and induction. You should spend about a month on each stage to ensure that you have everything in place to hire your VA extraordinaire. This is important, as having a VA extraordinaire is actually as much about you, and your relationship with your VA, as it is about them.

Preparation

Lots of people hire a VA without really knowing what they are going to do — they just vaguely feel like they need help moving away from the administrative tasks. This isn't the way to start a good relationship. The first month needs to be spent establishing what it is your VA is going to do for you, and what needs to be in place before recruiting to make it work.

You will need to consider:

- **Tasks:** The basis of everything is the actual stuff your VA is going to do. For 30 days you're going to carry a notebook and record everything that you are doing that your VA could do for you. Don't even think about hiring anyone until you have 52 tasks you want them to do for you.

- **Platforms:** There is a bunch of technical stuff you need to have in place in order to be able to communicate effectively with your offshore VA, to be able to manage them remotely, and to have the right stuff in the cloud. You need to know what these are and how to implement them yourself.

- **Job Description:** This document is the foundation for the relationship. You need to clearly state the position details (accountabilities, technical skills, personal skills) and the financial details (conditions, remuneration, structure).

Recruiting

Most of us aren't HR experts and don't know how to effectively recruit locally, let alone virtually. We need to be able to communicate who we are and what our needs are, as well as reliably assessing our potential VA's skills and character. This is not a time to rush, as the troubles of working with an unsuitable VA are far worse than spending a bit longer finding the right one. Just ask Pete about that! He's now got the extraordinary Cristina heading his VA team, but it took some time to find her. It's worth taking this part seriously.

Key elements of the recruiting process include:

- **Advertising:** If we want to get the best of the best, this is as much about selling your business as it is about saying what you want.

- **Selection:** How to pick which VA to hire? This involves a testing process, skills matrix, interview questions and an evaluation process.

- **Agreement:** Here you need a solid contract — how much to pay, how to handle leave, how to transfer money, what the '13th month' is (if your VA is based in the Philippines), health insurance, notice period, and all that stuff. Set it out clearly now and you won't have problems down the track.

Induction

This third month your focus should be on how to bring your Gun VA into the team and manage them going forwards. Actually putting aside the time to do this well is crucial — you can't expect your VA to be instantly familiar with your practice, let alone with you as a person. Remember, you're building a relationship here, and it's one that you want to support you for many years. Put the effort in to help your VA start well. Do that, and they'll be as passionate about your thought leadership as you are.

Issues to consider here are:

- **Kick-off:** The first week is critical, as you go through exactly what they should be doing for you in week one, and what you need to be doing to support them.

- **Manage:** Managing a virtual VA is different to managing someone sitting in the same office as you. You need to put systems in place so that you get the most out of your VA and have them feel like a valued part of the team.

- **Review:** Lastly, you need to manage performance reviews and salary reviews with the aim of having your Gun VA with you for the next ten years.

Find a Gun VA, and your day to day life will suddenly become exponentially easier, as they take over everything from booking travel, managing your diary, answering your phone, paying your bills, writing invoices and managing your programs. With this support in your team, you can get back to your work — being a thought leader.

5. Measure the right things

In your thought leadership practice there are four critical things to measure:

1. Your thinking

2. What you sell

3. What you deliver (remember your primary job is to think, sell and deliver)

4. The cash that comes in

Measuring your thinking is simply a case of counting how many IP Snapshots you start, and how many you complete to the point of a working version. A working version is something you are ready to use in a program (IP Snapshots are never complete — there is always the next version of your thinking).

When is a sale a sale? That's different for different people and different practices, and it's up to you to determine where the line is that clients need to cross. If you sell a future program and take a deposit, that could be when you count the sale. Alternatively, when you send an invoice that could be the time — if you have a high level of confidence that the invoice will get paid. With some clients, a verbal agreement might be sufficient. For public programs it is always when the payment is made. And it might be different for different clusters. You need to get clear what it is for you, and to measure it. If you ever count a sale that falls through (it happens to the best of us), make sure it comes off your scoreboard.

It is also critical to have effective systems for bringing in the money when you make a sale. For example, if you have a coaching program then get paid *before* you begin delivering the program, ideally via credit card so you are not sending invoices and chasing them up — especially for public programs. When someone books you for a keynote speech or a corporate workshop, get 50 per cent as a deposit, and ideally, the balance before the delivery. For a public training program, always get paid in full before the workshop. The income that you generate and collect is one of the truest measurements of the success of your practice. This is also the area many practitioners do not manage well, and this can lead to cash-flow shortages and challenging times as you wait for income to be deposited into your account.

By being proactive about obtaining payment up-front, and having these measurement systems in place, your attention can be on sales — not on chasing people for payment from sessions you delivered months ago.

Delivery is when you actually do the do. For a keynote address or a workshop this is obvious — it counts on the day when you show up and do your thing. If you sell a 12-month coaching program, the sale might be in one go up-front, but the delivery is spread out over the year; same with an online training program.

You want to be set up so that your delivery is efficient and effective. Efficient means that the preparation time is minimal: we package once and sell often. This means that if you are delivering a keynote speech that you've done before, it doesn't take much time to get ready to do it again. A coaching or mentoring session doesn't take a lot of time outside the actual session. What you measure is the amount of dollars you have delivered.

And finally, measure the cash. There is a saying in small business that cash is king, and it applies to your practice too. Always be on top of the cash flow — know each week how much cash has hit your bank account. And know how much you are owed, and when it is due. The shorter the amount of time between you doing the work and getting paid, the better — and if you can get paid before doing the work, that's ideal. If at all possible, don't put yourself in the position where either you are waiting 30, 60 or 90 days after delivering a program for payment, or where you or your team are putting time and energy into chasing money you are owed.

If your thinking has been done well, if your delivery is efficient and effective, and if you have good systems for bringing in the cash, it means you can turn your attention to selling. This is what will move you up the revenue ladder. Each day and each week you need to be thinking: 'What invitation can I give to whom that could end up in a sale?' There is a certain energy that comes with sales that effective sales teams have, but which many thought leaders have a resistance to. You want to get some of that energy into your practice, some of that hunger, and some of that mindset that you are going to hit your sales target no matter what. When you get to blue belt and above, your practice will start to have its own momentum, and you will have more and more people coming to you. However, at white belt it's time to put in the time and energy to get your practice going.

We recommend that you keep a log of what you sell and what you deliver every day. Then each week total up what you sold (in terms of how many dollars), what you delivered (likewise, how many dollars) and how much cash came in. Before you get to white belt your benchmark is $2,500 sold *and* delivered each week. Don't stop selling when you get busy delivering — you need to keep doing both. When you get to white belt, your benchmark is $5,000 a week sold and delivered. Because when you are selling, delivering and receiving $5,000 a week, that's $20,000 a month ongoing — and you're suddenly at yellow belt.

When you have gone beyond white belt, it's time to choose your next cluster. What's your next activity going to be? How will you take your practice to yellow belt? If you are mentoring a particular market with a particular message, could you offer a training program to the same market? Perhaps a different market would buy the same thing you are currently selling. Alternatively, it could be time to bring out a new message, and a new part of your IP.

Dr Sean Richardson

Dr Sean Richardson is a Canada-based thought leader who reached black belt in Australia and then moved his practice back to Canada.

Sean is a former elite athlete who not once but twice missed going to the Olympics with the Canadian rowing team after over-training and consequent injury. These experiences, combined with a decade of study and research into the field of sports psychology and the workings of the human mind, make Sean one of the world's foremost experts in high-performance mindsets and their application to excellence in teams, leaders, and individuals in business, professional sport, performing arts and life. Sean is passionate about coaching, training and mentoring people and teams to get the best out of themselves at the highest levels of performance.

Sean is also obsessed with understanding the things that stop people, and how to help them move through such challenges with resilient thinking. He works with corporates, performing artists and professional athletes doing this. In particular, he has worked in Melbourne, Australia, with the St Kilda Football Club (for those not from Australia, football in Melbourne is referred to as the local religion), transforming their culture and helping take them to the top of the ladder.

Sean's practice has been likened to 'Freud meets the Buddha and Michael Jordan at meditation/basketball boot camp'—deep understanding, non-judgment and high performance all in one!

Getting to white belt

Sean got to white belt by utilizing his expertise in resilience and mental toughness and performance psychologies. His thought leadership was seeded in both his deep academic training and his own experience as an elite athlete. When Sean started down the Thought

Leaders journey, he already had a small contract with a professional Australian Football League team — the St Kilda Football Club. By taking on the principles of a thought leaders practice, he was able to repackage and negotiate a contract through the football club that reflected the massive value he was providing. That contract was enough to get Sean to the white belt level of income.

The biggest challenge going from white belt to black belt

Sean's biggest challenge was shifting his market. He was successful in the professional sports market, but wanted to expand his practice into the corporate market. Having been an elite athlete, then working with the football club and working with elite athletes in an Olympic sport, Sean had the mindset that he was the 'sports guy', even though he had done some work in management consulting and had some contacts in the corporate world. He thought he wasn't really a corporate person as he couldn't 'speak their language', and wasn't that interested in corporate affairs. However, Sean *was* very interested in leadership and human behavior in any context (including the corporate world), although one of his barriers was the thought 'I don't really belong there'.

There were four key things that enabled Sean to overcome this challenge.

First, he stopped trying to come up with ideas that sounded corporate and started owning his space as a high-performance expert with experience in sport. He stopped trying to be someone else, and started being himself in a new environment. He became the 'high-performance guy' rather than the 'sports guy'. And what Sean discovered was that while business per se was new to him — the corporate world was an unfamiliar environment — the personalities didn't feel new. He found that dealing with a CEO or a CFO or an MD is the same as talking to a senior coach of an elite professional team. So, ironically, he felt completely at home, completely comfortable in that environment when he owned his expertise and went back to being himself. He wasn't trying to tell them how to run their business (which he isn't an expert in). He was working in the area that he *is* an expert in — human beings. Sean knows how they behave, how they respond to leadership, and how they respond to communication. Sean gets those subtle dynamics that occur between people, and that expertise is equally valuable in the corporate boardroom as it is on an elite sports field.

Second, Sean got very busy working on his IP — his ideas and his message. As he says, he was up at 2 o'clock, 3 o'clock in the morning, working on his first keynote speech and the potential ideas around training programs and mentoring opportunities that would flow from it. He developed the IP Snapshots and his ideas around mental toughness and resilience and what creates a high-performance culture. Because of the hard thinking he had done, he had that substance behind him, and he had a lot of conviction about the value he could offer.

Third, Sean then started sharing this with friends and associates — basically with anyone who would listen. He got it out of his head and off his computer and out into the world. That led to introductions, and very quickly Sean was doing a lot of keynote speeches and other work with corporate clients.

Finally, Sean had the confidence gained from implementing his IP with the St Kilda Football Club and knowing that his ideas really worked in the sporting environment. That gave Sean real conviction that what he had to share was valuable: it was the packaging through the IP Snapshot process and being able to present it in a way that appeared valuable to others that really gave Sean his first breakthrough in the corporate world with his own thought leadership.

The biggest mistake

Sean is an expert in resilience — he has this saying 'You win every game you lose'— if you have made a mistake, turn it into an opportunity. So it's ironic that Sean reports his biggest mistake as getting caught up in a perfectionist mentality, which meant that he didn't want to share what he was doing until he thought he'd got it just right. He kept thinking and refining his IP as an avoidance mechanism rather than getting out and selling it. And in the end, it took Sean months longer to get to market than he needed to — the program he had three months earlier would have really helped people back then, but he was still busy perfecting it. Which cost him time and money.

The difference that getting to black belt has made in Sean's life

At black belt Sean doesn't feel like he's working — he loves what he does. When he is developing his IP, he doesn't feel like he *has* to do it — he does it because it's what he enjoys. Sean loves nothing more than to go to Starbucks (remember, he's Canadian) and drink crappy coffee and do his thinking with pen and paper. He meets his clients in coffee shops and flies to conferences to talk to cool people about the stuff he's passionate about. He has been thinking about the ideas for years and is now able to share in a way that makes a big difference in the lives of others. As Sean says, definitely a labor of love!

Sean was also able to buy a house when he reached black belt. His wife was pregnant and he bought a house that he hadn't thought he would be able to afford until he was much older. It's given him and his family a sense of security, and it's also given Sean a real confidence in himself and his work.

Advice to someone starting out

Sean's advice to someone starting out on this journey is to work on the ability to be non-judgmental. People say they are going to do something, and they go out, and they try to do it, and then often they fail. For example, they say they are going to sell a program, so they put together some IP, they do their IP Snapshots, and after that first little bit of work they try to sell. And it fails, and they stop. They give up because they feel discouraged, and that discouragement comes from judgment of self. Non-judgment is being able to say at an internal level: 'It's probably normal that I failed.'

Expect to fail a lot in the beginning; the faster you can fail the better. It's not a measure of you as a person. It's a measure of feedback on your process, or your message, or your method. It could be a good indicator that you didn't get something right in the process, and if you're not sure how to clear that up then get some mentoring and find out.

Sean believes there is a real mindset shift that's important here to start off with, and it's understanding that this is a hard path in terms of the work that's required and the time and effort you put in. It starts with a sense of possibility — seeing that you can achieve this, that it's not impossible.

There is a very clear path forward here, and if you're committed and you see that possibility, you can achieve it.

15.

Yellow Belt

Price is what you pay. Value is what you get.

— WARREN BUFFET

Yellow belt is the second level on the Thought Leaders Revenue Ladder. Yellow belt corresponds to $20,000 a month or $240,000 a year from your practice. At this stage, your thought leadership practice should be generating more interest, repeat clients and an increase in your activity.

BELT	INCOME	FOCUS
5th Dan	$1,200,000	Distribution
4th Dan	$1,080,000	Capacity
3rd Dan	$960,000	Productivity
2nd Dan	$840,000	Engagement
Black Belt	$720,000	Investment
Red Belt	$600,000	Leverage
Blue Belt	$480,000	Positioning
Green Belt	$360,000	Activity
Yellow Belt	**$240,000**	**Value**
White Belt	$120,000	Decision

Also remember that, as with a martial art, the basics stay with you. So you don't stop doing the items discussed in white belt. The difference is that the focus now changes from *decision* to *value*.

FOCUS: VALUE

The focus for yellow belt is *value*. All the black belts we spoke to in preparing for this book talked about value — the importance of thinking in terms of value, of selling value and, of course, of delivering value.

The concept of value is very powerful because it takes us out of our own world and into that of our clients and our market. What will deliver value to them?

Often, when someone is an employee they are trained to think in terms of units of time. They trade their time for money; they get paid so much per hour, day, week or year, and provided they don't do anything too terrible they'll continue to get paid as long as they keep putting in the time.

A common pitfall for people achieving their yellow belt is falling into this same mindset. When speaking with people starting this journey, we often receive the following questions:

- How much can I charge per hour for my coaching or mentoring?

- What do other people charge?

- How much can I charge for a 45-minute keynote presentation?

- How much do people pay for a one-day training program?

It's as if people are programmed to think in terms of units of time — and they try to put a specific figure on that time. This is usually based on what they have heard others do, or what they feel will not get knocked back.

At yellow-belt level, you need to advance to think in terms of effort, knowledge and content. *'How much effort am I putting into this? How much of my blood, sweat and tears goes into this program? How much knowledge do I have and do I transfer? What is the content I am delivering?'*

The breakthrough comes when we think in terms of value. How much value will my client get from this offering? A great question that you could be asking is: *'For my client, how much will they save/ make/ create by implementing the information that I share with them?'*

Obviously, clients will invest more in items that will give them the opportunity for a better return. If you can deliver this value, they will understand the benefit of your thought leadership as well as actively promote your capabilities to others. Word-of-mouth referrals are much more powerful from someone who has received this value from you. When you add a tremendous amount of value, your clients achieve better results and promote you even more.

FIVE THINGS TO DO AT YELLOW BELT

1. Value your expertise

If you don't value your expertise, no one else will. However, often we are too close to our own thinking to really appreciate what we have come up with. We've been thinking about it and living with it for too long — we need to get some perspective on our IP to recognize its value. Again, you need to put yourself in the shoes of your client and value the difference you will make. Often this will require you to play a mental game with yourself that constantly reminds you of the value that you, as a thought leader, provide to others.

It's easy to have a limiting belief about how much expertise is worth. Many of us have grown up with parents who worked hard all their lives and earned modest incomes as employees. At the yellow-belt level, the amount you could be earning is to many what would be a reasonable annual salary — but earning it every quarter. This challenges the mindsets or limiting beliefs of what is or is not possible. It will push you up against all your mental barriers about money and about your self-worth, and it's a great opportunity to break through them both!

Valuing your expertise inspires you to keep thinking and keep working on your ideas and making them better. It also leads to the personal conviction and belief that others are looking for in a trusted advisor.

2. Value your time

As you move up the belts, you start to value your time differently. Yellow belt means selling and delivering $5,000 a week — $1,000 a day. Black belt is triple that: $15,000 a week sold and delivered. If your time is worth $1,000 a day, or that's what you are aspiring to be making at your next belt level, there are things that you should no longer be doing in your practice — things that value your time at less than that.

If your time is now worth $1,000 a day, then it no longer makes sense to do the $25-per-hour jobs in your practice. At this level, you now need to start thinking of how to more effectively leverage your time — and hand over some of the less important tasks to someone else.

When your income hits the yellow-belt level, it is probably time to turn your virtual assistant into a full-blown business manager.

Here's what the wonderful Elouise McCallum, Matt's business manager for many years, said about how a business manager is different from an executive assistant, and what to look for:

- A good relationship. The most important thing is a good working relationship.

- Not afraid of change. Needs to be someone who isn't looking for routine.

- Not attached to the work they have done. You can spend three months working on a project only to discover the market doesn't like it, and it gets dumped.

- Lots of initiative. The business manager runs the practice, so they can't need direction all the time — especially if you are away delivering your IP with clients regularly.

- Willing to sell. Not scared of making a sale (although Elle did say that that was something she learned on the job).

- Willing to embrace technology. This is key to leveraging your time and your activity and a business manager needs to be willing to learn how to set up and automate different forms of technology.

- Willing to take advice on how to perform the role better.

- Doesn't want to run a thought leaders practice themselves; isn't interested in the limelight, being on the stage, running the workshops.

It's a great summary of what to look for in your business manager.

3. Re-evaluate your prices ... and increase them

At yellow belt you are going to be busy, and as you move to green belt it's only going to get busier. Now is the time to move away from low-value work that you may have become comfortable with. A word of caution here. We know numerous people who have been too cautious or too aggressive in the way they deal with their pricing. We know of some trainers who made the decision to increase their fees from $1,500 a day to $5,000 a day and they starved, while others increased their rate by more and they flourished. What we noticed is that those who put their fees up successfully had built up a new cluster and began heavily promoting that — rather than suddenly doing a knee-jerk reaction and increasing fees to all of their current clients or in all of their markets.

Also, remember that the key is to focus on the value that you offer and what this is worth to other people. You need to have conviction that if what you are offering is of value, then people will be willing to invest in your expertise. Another question to ask yourself is, would *you* invest this amount in your offering? To get to black belt you will have to get comfortable charging amounts that some people think are outrageous.

Lifting the bar on what you charge also forces you to lift the bar on what you deliver, which is healthy for your practice. We find that this often forces you to continue upgrading your offering, which keeps you on the leading edge rather than being someone who always delivers the same message in the same way over and over.

Don't get caught up in the cycle of charging the same amount to the same client for the same offering over and over. It often does not help you — or them. We can tend to hang on to clients because we think they need us, even if they can't afford to pay us our current rates. This is, in effect, providing charity.

Within your thought leadership practice, be commercial. Don't do low-value work. Recognize that the more low-value work you hang on to, the harder it is to move up the belts.

Now is the time to finish up engagements that are bringing in less money than is appropriate for your current level and the value you provide. This is difficult to do — as is turning down work at lower rates. We have to trust that we will keep getting work, that the clients won't run out. If you have worked on your message, your marketing approach and your cluster offerings, then this is simply having faith in your offer.

Often there is a fear that things will dry up, and we feel that we need to hang on tightly to everything that comes our way. Whilst this fear is a natural consideration, if we can't get past it we'll make decisions that keep us from moving forward.

4. Build a communication platform

Having built an effective database, it is now time to design an effective communication platform. If you were a large company, you would have communications experts within your marketing department to create your strategic communication plan to nurture the relationships with clients and prospects.

In your practice, this is your job. The importance of it is often underestimated. What do you communicate, when, and to whom? Old-school hard sales are about getting a prospect to buy when you want to sell. An effective communication platform is about being there when they are ready to buy.

Look at all the different markets and segments within your database, and decide how you want to provide value and nurture your relationships with each of them.

A good starting point is a newsletter that you send out fortnightly or monthly, containing valuable content that people would be happy to receive. A weekly blog is another good idea. Creating your IP Snapshots will make both of these tasks easier.

Social media increasingly need to be part of your communication platform. How are you going to use LinkedIn, Twitter, Facebook, and other sources of social media? Likewise, video is becoming more important — creating video blogs is another powerful strategy.

5. Foster your network of like-minded thought leaders

One of the challenges for many individuals running a practice is that they often work in isolation. They are on their own, and need to foster their own idea stimulation as well as source new strategic initiatives. We have known some amazing thought leaders who became lonely and demotivated and gave up their practice because of the lack of stimulation — or the lack of any strong community to help challenge and grow their ideas.

One of the reasons for forming the Thought Leaders movement was to create a community where really clever people could hang out and share ideas that are commercially smart. Imagine a place where you could be recognized for your expertize and still be in awe of the others around you. We view this community as creating two critical components necessary for any infopreneur to be successful: knowledge and network.

Stimulating minds coming together help to stretch conventional thinking. We have participated in numerous Thought Leaders conferences where a participant shared an idea that was a critical next step for someone else in the room. The innovation and ideas that are openly shared create a fountain of knowledge that others can drink from.

The network gives you a sense of connection with others who are on the same journey. Given that many thought leaders run their practices from home, this touch point provides the interaction that is often missing in their success. It will often allow you to identify others who may help you along your journey, and vice versa.

Once you have focused on the value that you offer, your business should begin to grow further. This is what it will take to get you to green belt. However, these are still just the early stages of the journey. Many people have got to this level and have stalled because they did not stay active enough to break through to green belt.

BLACK BELT UNDER THE MICROSCOPE

Rowdy McClean

Imagine starting a business at the age of 24 and competing with one of Australia's largest conglomerates — and being so successful that you could retire 10 years later. That is what Rowdy McClean did. He then moved on to become a CEO who has turned around ailing companies, before finally establishing a thought leadership practice. Rowdy has proved that by getting your attitude equation right, anything is possible.

Through his practice, he has spent the past decade inspiring individuals, teams and organizations to 'get things done', 'embrace and adapt to change' and 'execute on ideas' through focusing on their attitude.

To Rowdy, attitude is not about painting a rosy colored picture over a bleak canvas; it's about developing a constructive and resilient approach to business, culture, leadership, sales, service and teamwork.

His challenge to us all is to 'play a bigger game'.

Retiring at 34

As a young man Rowdy had two goals: he had a desire to have a million dollars in the bank, and he wanted to retire before he was 40. Rowdy retired at 34. His retirement only lasted six months as he became bored and wanted to do something to make a difference. His vision of retirement had been having the opportunity to do whatever he wanted, whenever he wanted — complete freedom. And initially he thought that doing it at 34 was pretty awesome. But what he found in the next six months was that just because he had freedom, it didn't mean that everybody else had freedom as well. So he'd play golf, but he was playing golf with others who were 74 years old, many of whom he did not know. All his friends were at work.

He'd go to the beach and there was nobody around, so he'd get really bored because there was nobody to share his time with.

It drove his wife insane, because if anybody did show up — and generally it was his family — Rowdy was intense and in-your-face. His kids would say: 'What is he on!' His wife ended up telling him 'I don't care what you do, but you need to go and find a job or do something.'

Rowdy was headhunted to run a hospitality business that had just lost a million dollars and sacked 150 staff. He had never worked in hospitality before, but he turned the business around in 12 months, then went on to increase their profits every year for the next six years.

Getting to white belt

During the time running the hospitality business, and because of the rapid turnaround he led, he was frequently asked to speak at events. Rowdy remembers speaking at one event and ending up having a mind-altering conversation with one of the other speakers. The speaker was saying how fantastic it all was — the conference was exciting, the hotel, the beach and the food were all sensational, and he got paid to be there. And Rowdy thought, 'Hello, I'm not getting paid to be here, what's going on?' That's when he started to explore the speaking side of thought leadership, and launched his practice.

He got to white belt in his practice through a combination of speaking and training. When he finished at the hospitality business he started a training company by default. He'd go and have a cup of coffee with some people he knew in the hospitality business. They would tell him about a pain-point they were experiencing, and he would sell them a solution that he didn't have at the time. He would then work like crazy to build the model and the materials so that he could fulfill on the promise he had made. The combination of that training with delivering keynote addresses got Rowdy through white belt very quickly.

The main challenges between white belt and black belt

The biggest challenge for Rowdy was reducing the number of delivery days so that he still had the freedom to 'play'. Given that he had already retired, he never intended to work full-time in his practice; but he got to the stage where he was absolutely flat out doing the amount of days that were maximum for him, and doing all the other tasks to keep the practice going. He overcame this challenge by setting up a team and systems to run his business so he could focus primarily on delivering keynote speeches and the training programs that he enjoys.

A big thing for Rowdy has been to keep visiting his core message. At first it was 'Get off your ass', which worked really well. He was paid well to do both the training and the speaking part of that. Then he took his thinking to another level, and his message became all about attitude.

Rowdy's next iteration was 'Play a bigger game', and he loves the continual search for depth. And he is sure that there is another shift in focus on the horizon — he just doesn't know what it is yet. He uses this continual refinement of his IP development to continue adding new content for his clients.

A million-dollar day

Rowdy has a program called 'Get Real' where he runs a full-day motivational seminar priced at $990 per person. He has run these in every capital city in Australia and one in New Zealand as well. One of these seminars made a quarter of a million dollars alone.

People might think that it's about the money, but actually it's not. For Rowdy it's about playing the game. He is now playing the game for a million-dollar day.

That sounds pretty outrageous, but Rowdy doesn't think it is if the people who are in that room walk away with an experience that changes their life. It doesn't matter whether it's one million or ten million if the people in the room say 'I've had an absolutely sensational event.' It's not about conning 1,000 people to come into a room and pay $990. It's about creating so much value in that $990 that each one of those people walks away feeling it was the best day they've ever had, and in hindsight would have gladly paid double for!

Advice to someone starting out

Rowdy's advice is first and foremost to invest in yourself. There is a lot of really good mentoring or training you can do that will help you lift your value. You might be doing something now where you're talking for $1,000 or running a program for $3,000 — so invest in taking it to the next level. Find a mentor or a training program that will enable you to lift those numbers. Rowdy believes that if you stop investing then you tread water. If he hadn't stumbled across the Thought Leaders concept, he might still have got to the $10,000 days and then the $30,000 days, but there's no way he would have got there as quickly as he did. He strongly believes that the more you learn, the more you earn.

His final words are that every time you put a number to paper or discuss a goal or a target with somebody, up the ante a little bit — play a bigger game and just see how far you can push yourself.

16.

Green Belt

If you always put limits on everything you do, physical or anything else, it will spread into your work and your life. There are no limits. There are only plateaus, and you must not stay there, you must go beyond them.

— BRUCE LEE

Green belt is the third level on the Thought Leaders Revenue Ladder. Green belt corresponds to $30,000 a month or $360,000 a year from your practice.

BELT	INCOME	FOCUS
5th Dan	$1,200,000	Distribution
4th Dan	$1,080,000	Capacity
3rd Dan	$960,000	Productivity
2nd Dan	$840,000	Engagement
Black Belt	$720,000	Investment
Red Belt	$600,000	Leverage
Blue Belt	$480,000	Positioning
Green Belt	**$360,000**	**Activity**
Yellow Belt	$240,000	Value
White Belt	$120,000	Decision

This is where you hit what we call the 'ceiling of exhaustion'. And where, strangely enough, you're busier and working harder than at any other time in your practice. As we mentioned previously, this is where you may have three plates (or clusters) spinning at the same time. You are constantly moving between these spinning plates to keep them moving — without letting them stall or fall off. For many thought leaders this level is often one of the most challenging to break through. However, once you do, your practice will begin to gain a new forward momentum.

FOCUS: ACTIVITY

The focus at green belt is *activity*. Do more stuff. Think more, sell more and deliver more. Work harder. Push through.

For anyone who has worked in the corporate sector and who had an insanely busy time putting in 60–70 hours per week, this will become familiar territory. One way to think of it is as if you are pushing a heavy 2-metre-diameter ball up a hill. Once you get it moving, because of its weight you cannot afford to stop the upward momentum; otherwise, it will begin to roll back down and you will have lost ground — not to mention the effort required to get it moving in the right direction again!

At green belt, the message is 'work harder'. The next level, blue belt, is when life starts to get easier, when your practice has enough momentum to be self-sustaining, and when the money goes up but the exertion goes down. But what it takes to get there is more work.

Lots of people give up at green belt. They hit the 'ceiling' and, exhausted, they then drop back to yellow. It's a challenging time in your practice, because you are probably working harder than you ever have before, and yet you know you need to do more. Think of it like getting back into fitness — first it gets harder!

We make the mistake of thinking that black belt will be twice as much work as green belt — which is clearly impossible — and so we think it can't be done. For many thought leaders, running a black belt practice is easier than running a green belt practice. Green belt is when you are working the hardest in your practice. You need to structure your life to maintain the activity without falling apart, and then continue the push through to blue belt.

FIVE THINGS TO DO AT GREEN BELT

1. Cancel all fun

A common recommendation is that you 'cancel all fun' until you hit blue belt, and then have your fun funded. Black belt Darren Hill reported that before blue belt he packed away his TV to eliminate the distraction from his work.

When you get to green belt, prepare yourself and the people in your life for a period of dedicated focus on your practice. Eliminate as many distractions as possible. What, for you, is the equivalent to packing away your TV? What are the things in your life that you can postpone in order to put the hard yards into your practice and break through to blue belt?

For many thought leaders, this means absolute focus on activity that will grow their practice. It often means that other things will need to be placed on a shelf to come back to later. This can be a tricky balance if you have a family as well as close friends. We have often heard those close to us mention how busy we have been or how often we have been travelling for work. This appears to be a common theme at this level.

One Thought Leaders Mentor had this to say:

As a green belt I had a three-week 'holiday' in Bali. Well, my wife had a holiday; I just did my work somewhere else. I had one day off while we were there, and the rest of the time I was putting in the work — doing just as much as I do in Australia. Just doing it somewhere a bit warmer, a bit cheaper, and closer to a pool.

One final note. In cancelling all fun, we don't mean not to look for fun in what you are doing. This is often the necessary stress-relief valve that can help you get through this level. Just don't plan on mentally checking-out for a long period of time!

2. Maintain your energy platforms

Running a practice as a thought leader takes endurance. One of the things that you need to ask yourself when you are making the decision to go for black belt is whether you currently have the stamina and endurance to go the distance. It's a marathon, not a sprint. You need to stay fit to get there. Looking after your body, your health and your energy is a critical component of managing your practice, especially at green belt.

Nutrition and diet are key. It is very easy for the quality of our diet to decrease as our activity increases. This is exactly the time when we need to increase the quality of what we put into our mouths. There are lots of great books and thought leaders on this very subject which go way beyond the scope of this book, but we will say a few things. Pretty much everyone would do well to increase the amount of fruit and vegetables in their diet. If your breakfast is predominantly fruit and your lunch and dinner is predominantly vegetables, you are well on the way to a sustaining, nutritious diet. You think better if you are properly hydrated, so make sure you drink water whenever you are thirsty. Similarly, most people would do better with fewer grains (particularly processed wheat), less dairy, fewer artificial foods (any additive that's identified by a number), less processed food and definitely less sugar.

Exercise is also critical for your thinking, your energy, and the sustainability of your practice. Ideally, your exercise regimen will include cardio, strength, and flexibility training. At the very least, make sure you do 30 minutes of exercise that gets your heart rate up four times a week. For many thought leaders, once they reach green belt they are constantly out travelling, spending numerous nights in hotels in different cities around the world. Be careful not to use this as an excuse not to maintain your diet and exercise regimen — it isn't one.

You and your body also need rest and relaxation. Make sure you are sleeping properly — most people need at least seven hours sleep a night to avoid sleep deprivation and to function optimally. Likewise, we need relaxation and downtime. Elite athletes train in cycles — they will generally have three intense weeks followed by a lighter week. Similarly, in our practice we need to balance out our intense periods with quality relaxation and downtime.

3. Speak more — and create a new distribution channel

Even if speaking isn't one of your delivery modes for income, now is the time to hone your speaking skills, and the best way to do that is by speaking. As you move through blue belt to black belt, you will be called upon more and more to speak in front of large groups. As a thought leader, speaking is a very smart way to get your message out. We have also found that there are two common considerations you need to be aware of, and to choose which is best for you: speaking for a fee or speaking for free.

Speaking for a fee is very straightforward. A client is interested in the message that you have to offer and wants you to 'tell' the audience this message. If you master the skills that we explain in detail on the speaking modality in the 'Your method' chapter, you can deliver this presentation to a standing ovation and a client who happily pays you for your time.

Speaking for free is a different strategy, aimed at distribution. A distribution keynote is a presentation that you develop to sell other offerings — that is, you don't make money out of the talk itself, you make money out of what you invite people to engage with when you deliver the talk. It's key in this example that you actually *do* invite them to engage with you.

4. Write more

Writing is another great green-belt activity, and something that you will keep doing as you move up through the belts as a thought leader. When someone writes something and publishes it to the world, it often establishes them as an expert. We do not mean just books. When someone starts blogging, tweeting, writing e-zines and putting their ideas out there, people take notice.

Many thought leaders are often surprised when others mention to them that they were inspired by the words that they wrote. Often, when capturing these thoughts and sending them out, we do not know who will read them, or how influential they might become.

Michael Henderson had this experience when he started writing more:

> When I wrote my first book it was to provide my clients with a resource to assist them without me. What it actually did was help me clarify my thoughts and more importantly position me as the expert. By publishing my ideas, it forced me to create and refine them to a level that others could understand — and I could leverage.

Again, even if you are not making money from it, now is a good time to start writing white papers and special reports. You could also offer to submit articles to specific magazines around your area of expertise. Although you might not make any money from this, it helps establish you as an expert and positions you as well. There are great promotional resources available, and these will give you a head-start when you get to blue belt and are purposefully looking for resources to position yourself as an expert.

5. Fail fast

In a thought leadership practice, you need to be willing to fail things quickly and cheaply. Part of the dance of building your practice is regularly coming up with new project clusters and taking them to market.

As you get more experienced you get a better idea of what the market will and won't want, but even the best of us don't know until we actually test it.

Many people have a fear of trying something until it is perfect or completely finished. When running a thought leadership practice, this often leads to a cycle of work and rework on a concept or an idea. This is not useful activity and will not help you move forward! Rather than spending six months developing something that you don't know whether people will buy, test it first. Sell it, and if people are interested enough to buy it, then develop it.

Remember to fail fast! If it doesn't fly, then move on. Don't invest much time, money or energy until you know that the idea is going to have some traction and make some money. Of course, you have to do this with integrity. Don't sell something unless you are confident that you can deliver on the outcomes. If you are working in the corporate world, the word gets out very quickly regarding who does and who does not have the capability to deliver on what they promise.

Domonique Bertolucci

Domonique Bertolucci is the bestselling author of *Your Best Life* and *The Happiness Code*. Born in Australia, Domonique's first career as a fashion model took her to London at the age of 22 where, realizing that she was never going to be a 'waif', she underwent a different type of extreme makeover: from model to corporate high-flyer. After 10 years in the corporate sector, where she earned a reputation for turning around underperforming teams, Domonique established her practice delivering a range of personal development programs to both the general public and companies. She now divides her time between Sydney and London.

Domonique is highly sought after as a professional speaker and is regularly engaged by a wide variety of organizations to deliver keynote presentations and seminars. In these she challenges her audience to think about what it is they really want from life, and explains the issues many people have that stop them from living the life they want.

Since the launch of *Your Best Life*, Domonique has built a reputation as the go-to person for quotes, comments and expert insights on what 'real' success is and how to achieve it — more than 10 million people have seen, read or heard her advice.

Getting to white belt

One of the early challenges for Domonique was the temptation to get a job in banking when she and her husband moved from London back to Australia. Although there was the attraction of retaining a huge banking income, Domonique knew that trying to start her coaching practice as well as holding a full-time job would not work. She believes that one of the reasons salaries are so large in banking is that it's so time-consuming — the job buys your body and your soul.

So she decided to make it all about what she wanted the future to look like. One problem many people face when they move into a practice is selling themselves and claiming their worth. Domonique never had any conflict about her worth because she knew what the banks would have been happy to pay her, and her thought was that her clients were getting a bargain.

Domonique didn't have any experience in building a practice from scratch. She had a lot of experience coming into very well-established organizations and creating new things for them or turning things around that weren't working. Domonique had done a lot of turnaround work with large, multi-multi-million-pound organizations, but this was completely different to starting her own practice.

Domonique found that within her personal network there were enough connections to get great contracts, so that she had reached white belt within two months and had a really good income within six months.

Given how successful she was, Domonique became extremely busy and was about to get stuck into more of the same activity when her husband, who had worked in sales, recommended that she start focusing on business development. Although she initially resisted his advice, she knew that he was right and decided to spend the following six months with one client, making much less money than she had in her first six months but all the time focusing on growing her practice.

A practice rather than a business.

Because of her success, many people have pushed Domonique to expand her practice and begin employing other people to deliver her approach. However, she sees this as a common mistake people make. Rather than building something just to make it bigger, she realized the challenges that many people have in managing 10–20 full-time staff and the impact that has on their business — and their life. She was very inspired when she joined the Thought Leaders community and was introduced to so many others who were running a practice rather than a business — and making just as much money whilst having the free time as well!

Main challenges

When Domonique looks back at her investment-to-earnings ratio and therefore at her return on investment in those first few years, the numbers were all way out of whack. She was far too caught up thinking 'build it and they will come'. On one hand, she didn't want to have a small-business mindset and create the expectation that everything was going to be a struggle without much money. On the other hand, she had to recognize that the dynamic of her enterprise was small.

In the first couple of years she found herself spending way too much. Because she'd been in an environment where the numbers were so huge, it felt like really small amounts of money to her. She needed to recognize that she was small, and make decisions in a size and budget-appropriate way. At the same time, she had to keep thinking really big, keep considering her massive dreams, and keep being audacious. Domonique found this tension to be a real challenge. It was something that took her a long time to get right. When she looks at the way she runs her practice now, she sees that she would have so much more money had she got that balance right a lot earlier.

Domonique invested heavily in things that she really shouldn't have been spending money on until she was much further up the revenue ladder. And when she should still have been in activity, she was giving a lot of work to alliances and paying a full-time PA for far more hours than she needed. When she got to the end of that particular financial year she had turned over a really high figure, but she'd paid out nearly half of what she'd earned in fees to alliances, partners, and business support. Again, the ratios were just wrong. That was another one of the big lessons that Domonique learned along the way.

Advice to someone starting out

Domonique's advice is to think big, spend small and invest wisely. Think big — but don't spend big. That doesn't mean skimping — just investing very wisely when you do spend money. Domonique will readily spend money on her personal and professional development, but not necessarily on having a state-of-the-art telecommunication system or an expensive office.

As she says:

> Continue to think big and believe that it's possible. But spend small — don't spend money you don't have, because you've got a practice. You're not building a business and you don't want to have a lot of overheads. Invest your time wisely, invest your money wisely and invest your energy wisely.

The paradox when you're starting out is that you need to have a black-belt mindset right from the start, so you need to be thinking like a black belt, but taking the activities and having the focus and the actions that are appropriate for the belt level that you are actually on regarding the revenue model.

The difference getting to black belt has made

Getting to black belt was incredibly liberating for Domonique — proving that she could do it, that there was actually enough money flowing through her practice so she could invest wisely, develop the programs she wanted, and get the support she wanted.

She describes it in this way:

> Success breeds success. And the more successful you feel, the more successful you become; the bigger you are, the more in demand you'll be; the more that's going on, the more people will want you to get involved in their business and their lives.

17.

Blue Belt

Blue belt is the fourth level on the revenue model, and — you'll be pleased to learn! — it's the point when it actually starts to get easier. At blue belt, your practice starts to have its own momentum, and the experience is one of being in flow. Prior to blue belt you needed to put more energy out to bring revenue in; now it starts to be the other way around. Your practice starts to have its own attraction and will continue to grow as long as you focus on positioning.

BELT	INCOME	FOCUS
5th Dan	$1,200,000	Distribution
4th Dan	$1,080,000	Capacity
3rd Dan	$960,000	Productivity
2nd Dan	$840,000	Engagement
Black Belt	$720,000	Investment
Red Belt	$600,000	Leverage
Blue Belt	**$480,000**	**Positioning**
Green Belt	$360,000	Activity
Yellow Belt	$240,000	Value
White Belt	$120,000	Decision

FOCUS: POSITIONING

Positioning is about amplifying the attractive part of your business, and that's our focus at blue belt — activities and projects that position you as the authority in your field.

You want to get to the point where your name will always come up when someone is looking to do something in your area. The conversation will be: 'You have to talk to (insert your name here) before you go any further!'

This is at the core of being a thought leader, a recognized subject-matter expert in a particular area. When you have this area of expertise identified, the blue-belt level is about developing strategies to ensure that everyone else knows that you hold this position in the marketplace. Often it is not a case of who you know; it is more a case of who knows you. Who knows about you as the expert in a particular area? There are thousands of trainers offering training to clients. How does someone know who would be the best for them and who has had a successful track record with others? Positioning is a key point of difference. It is what separates you from all the other trainers out there. More importantly, effective positioning sets you up as a specific thought leader in the field, whilst leaving all of the others as 'just another trainer'. This is not to say that other trainers don't have incredible abilities; it is just that they haven't positioned themselves as more than just a trainer.

One important thing to be aware of is that your positioning needs to establish you as a *thought leader* — not just as a role title. Remember, you should never position yourself as only one of a speaker, trainer, coach, author, facilitator or mentor. If you want to grow your income and reach black belt and beyond, you need to move across all the modes in your offerings. Your positioning must be larger than any one of these roles.

We have also noticed that this is often the stage when people focus more on ensuring that everything which has their name or brand on it stays *in palette*. By 'in palette' we mean that every piece of collateral is consistent and has the same feel. This means that your visuals, handouts, email banner, marketing materials and website all support this same consistent feel. You have been running so hard to date that some things are still first-generation — bring everything up to the latest. This is an activity that you need to do from time to time in your fast-moving, project-driven practice. It's like a brand tune-up after a series of fast races.

Many thought leaders also take this further than physical objects, to include themselves and the way they look. Often this involves using an image consultant to help ensure that your physical image is congruent with your brand image. One Thought Leaders Mentor described this experience as his 'pretty-woman day', where he spent a day with an image consultant who helped him to completely change his wardrobe to ensure it was on brand — and, more importantly, positioned him as an expert. As Thought Leaders Ambassador Peter Sheahan, author of *FL!P* and *Making It Happen* often says, *"Superficial is anything but!"*

FIVE THINGS TO DO AT BLUE BELT

1. Brand you — what are you going to be famous for?

Tom Peters is the poster-child for successful thought leadership, and of course has achieved far beyond black belt. His practice makes money through the top four modes: speaking, authoring, training and mentoring. He has written more than a dozen international best-selling books and delivered over 2,500 keynote speeches to almost three million people. He is constantly refining his thinking and his brand. His message has evolved as he has. He originally hit the big time with his first (co-authored) book *In Search of Excellence* in the early 1980s. How he promoted that was a piece of positioning genius.

Tom had been working as a consultant for McKinsey, and he printed out 1,000 copies of the manuscript and sent them to everyone he knew. This was before the days of self-publishing—today, he would have simply sent them all their own copy of the book. He had already been nurturing his database. Because the book was so good (revolutionary, in fact), it created a buzz even before it was published. He hasn't looked back.

Peters has since recognized that within the corporate world it is critical for professionals to build their own brand and their own positioning independent of the company they work for. He has coined the phrases 'Brand You' and 'You Inc' to describe this. Likewise, Peter Sheahan (one of the case study examples in this book), has also mastered positioning himself using a brand—not just once, but twice—before he turned 30!

Michael Gerber, in his book *The E-Myth*, talks about the imperative in a business to get your name off the door. In a practice it's the exact opposite—it's imperative to get your name *on* the door. Positioning 'you' as the brand is even more important in a practice. As a thought leader, your practice is built around *you* and the ideas that *you* generate.

Think back to the chapter on your message. What is it that you want to be known for? In ten years' time, what do you want your name to be synonymous with? What is the contribution that you want to make with your thought leadership?

Now is the time to start positioning you and your name and your brand towards that goal. Ideally you have yourname.com as your shop front with your name on the door. If someone else has got that, it's almost worth changing your name—but not quite. Get as close as you can—include a middle initial or a hyphen, or go for .net or a local url. Then use it to position yourself as the expert in your field. For examples go to mattchurch.com, petercook.com, or scottstein.com.au.

2. Get your book published

Now is the time to get your book written and published. Unless you are Tom Peters, you won't actually make money from the sale of your book. People are so trained to paying $25–$35 for a 250-page business book that it is almost impossible to charge anything else. A typical agreement with a major publisher is a 10 per cent royalty on the recommended retail price. That means that for every book sold you might make $2–$3. So even if 10,000 copies are sold, that is only $20,000–$30,000 in income. Hardly enough to make you rich.

So why write a book? It is the ultimate piece of positioning. If you have written a book, suddenly you are the expert. It gives you instant credibility, even if it's not deserved. Being an author makes it much more likely that you will be booked for keynote addresses, that people will come to your training events, and that they will hire you for mentoring, facilitating and training. In short, it sells all your other modes.

Another thought around publishing a book is to self-publish. This is another strategy that thought leaders use to get their ideas into print without having to wait to work around a publisher's typical timetable. Advantages of this approach are that you can fast track the time it takes to publish a book and you control the price and profit from each book. Depending on the book, self-publishing can cost you anywhere between $4 and $10 per book to produce. Be aware that you will need a strategy to fund this cost as well as having an effective distribution model to sell the books. White belt is too early to be spending all of this money on one marketing format when you are still growing your practice.

3. Collaborate with other experts

Collaboration with other experts is an extremely powerful and often under-utilized positioning strategy. When you collaborate with someone who already has a strong position and brand in your target market, that rubs off on you. Paradoxically, it is also good for them — working with other experts strengthens their positioning too.

Thought leader Darren Hill is a master of this strategy. He has turned Darwin, a tiny city in the tropical north of Australia between the desert and the ocean, into his own town. A big part of how he has done that has been to bring in other experts from the rest of Australia to speak on his stage. Rather than being threatened by the people who were currently more successful and had more of a track record than him, he collaborated with them, paid for them to come to Darwin, and put them in front of his people. And his people loved him for it. They saw the caliber of people that Darren was hanging out with, and related to him (and paid him) accordingly. Of course, it wasn't long before Darren was a black belt himself and doing the same for other thought leaders around the country.

Think about who already has the position in the market you want, and collaborate with them. Invite them in to talk to your people, run a program with them, be seen on the same stage as them, and pay them to come to your events.

4. Take a leadership position within your community

Taking a leadership position within your professional bodies is another simple yet effective positioning strategy. If you are a member of a coaching association or speakers' association or trainers' body, then become actively involved in these associations. It could be in an official role such as president or a specific chairperson, or it could be to offer to present and share your expertise with others at their annual conferences or meetings. Both strategies can be effective in you being recognized by others for your area of thought leadership. Often, if they know and respect you and they are not able to work with a client that needs a particular set of skills, they will refer you to the client instead.

Some associations that you could get involved with include:

For speakers

- Global Speakers Federation, www.globalspeakers.net
- National Speakers Association in the USA, www.nsaspeaker.org
- Professional Speakers Australia, www.professionalspeakers.org.au

For authors

- The International Association of Writers, www.associationofwriters.com
- Australian Society of Authors, www.asauthors.org

For trainers

- American Society for Training & Development in the USA, www.astd.org or in Australia, www.astd.org.au
- Australian Institute of Training and Development, www.aitd.com.au

For mentors

There does not appear to be a large community or association yet that fits into our definition of mentoring (most of them re-package coaching). There is, of course, the Thought Leaders Mentor community and the Thought Leaders Mentors who have completed this journey before and who share their wisdom. The Mentors have completed Thought Leaders Business School and now Mentor other thought leaders. To find out more go to www.tlbusinessschool.com.

For facilitators

- International Association of Facilitators, www.iaf-world.org

For coaches

- International Coaching Federation, www.coachfederation.org

5. Get media coverage: traditionally or via social media

Getting media coverage to position you as a thought leader is an important step for any blue belt. It allows you to be positioned as a person of authority and gets people to remember who you are — and hopefully refer you or your ideas to others.

Traditionally, this involved using the resources of a public relations firm. They specialize in getting people into the media and using their network of contacts to position key products, services or people. This could involve something as simple as opening doors to put you in touch with newspaper editors for you to submit articles for printing, or putting together a full-blown PR campaign designed to get you to front-of-mind of your target audience or a marketplace. This could cost anywhere from $5,000 for a specific project, to $5,000–$10,000 per month, depending on the size of the campaign. Be careful not to over-capitalize too early, and make sure that you track the effectiveness of any PR activity.

Sites such as Facebook, Twitter, LinkedIn, Google+ and YouTube provide social media platforms that allow people to position themselves as thought leaders. It is important to recognize that just having a Facebook page does *not* equate to having a social media strategy. To effectively position yourself, you need a range of initiatives on a range of social platforms that continuously broadcast your position as an authority to the masses.

Darren Hill

Nothing about Darren's journey to black belt is typical. Prior to establishing his practice, Darren spent a decade working in an abattoir followed by a few years as a bouncer at bars. He also managed a multimillion-dollar hotel before entering public service to manage a tourism and hospitality college.

Despite this, Darren unlocked his own passion for lifelong learning and proceeded to put himself through university whilst working full-time, resulting in a psychology degree and a postgraduate qualification in Management Communications.

He also established his black-belt practice in the unlikeliest of locations — Darwin. Darwin is a small city (or a large town, depending on who you talk to) in the tropical north of Australia, more famous for its crocodiles and hurricanes, and for being bombed in World War II, than as a commercial hub.

Darren is obsessed with humanizing workplaces, and through speaking, authoring and training he aims to assist a new wave of leadership based on the one common denominator at work: our human skills.

Getting to white belt

The first step to getting to white belt is quite simply making the decision. For a while Darren had been thinking about leaving his job and heading into his own employment — he probably spent 12–18 months ruminating over the decision. He truly believes that just making the decision and going for it was the most critical thing to getting to that $10,000 a month.

One of the key strategies Darren used was to box up his TV. He actually took his TV and put it back in its cardboard box for the three months leading into starting his practice. When Darren got home from work, he just sat down and started working on his IP. That was why Darren launched so well and got to white belt almost immediately. To start with, he aimed at the low-hanging fruit. Darren had worked for a number of years in federal government agencies, so he targeted other government agencies. He knew there was a shortage of good training so he put together his training offering and just targeted that one market.

His main challenges

Darren's first challenge was understanding his value and overcoming the self-limiting beliefs that were holding him back — the voice in the back of his head saying 'I'm not as good as I think I am.' Darren had to really step into that space where he had conviction that he was offering a great-value proposition to a market and that clients would be much better off by engaging him.

The second challenge for Darren was concentrating on what he's good at. A couple of times he diverted from his expertise and headed off to chase what he thought were greener pastures, and every time it backfired. Darren's success, particularly during the early stages of the revenue ladder, came from sticking to what he knew like the back of his hand, and staying consistent with one or two messages to a couple of very specific markets.

Successful strategies

Positioning, positioning, positioning. Darren has seen many thought leaders hit the activity cycle around green belt, and it either breaks them or they back off from it because it's all such hard work. Getting to $360,000 a year is hard work — you can find yourself doing lots of hours. For a lot of us, we set up our practice because we want a better lifestyle — and all of a sudden we find ourselves at green-belt level and we're doing 80-hour weeks. It's then that positioning is critical.

We're really lucky within the Thought Leaders community that there are great experts to position with. Darren firmly believes that you can't position or re-position yourself without assistance — particularly to a market that already knows you. A great fast track to re-positioning yourself in a market that already knows you is to bring in talent and work alongside that talent. All of a sudden that same customer thinks: 'I never knew he hung out with people like that, I never knew he carried such weight.'

Darren also learned early on that when he got asked to join different networking groups, it was better to say that he was happy to come along and speak rather than become a member. He still gave them some of his knowledge and his IP, but it positioned him beyond the group — and positioned him much more effectively than being a member. It is also a much more leveraged use of Darren's time to show up once as the star rather than turn up every week.

Advice to someone starting out

Consider what currencies you are accepting for your services and your expertise in lieu of money — especially psychological payoffs, or boosts to your ego.

We all have a number of different currencies in our life, whether it's being liked, or acceptance from our peers, or approval. Sometimes we've got to check our currencies, because if we are wanting to make money we really need to examine what other currencies are at play. Darren has observed some people on the speaking circuit, for example, who are high-volume speakers doing 200 presentations in a year but they're only charging $1,000 or $2,000; and they're looking at other speakers who are charging $6,000 or $10,000 a speech and they're wondering how they do that. But their 'currency' is that they want to be seen as being heavily booked. Darren would prefer to speak 20 times a year if he got paid $10,000 each time versus speaking 200 times at $1,000. But for some people, the lure of being seen as heavily booked and being able to say 'I picked up 15 gigs this week' is a very big currency.

Darren keeps coming back to what's most important, what's the biggest currency. He knows that in his life with his young family and where he wants to head to, money's a big currency. He gets plenty of love and acceptance from his kids and his wife, so he doesn't need to get that out in the marketplace. He has learned to drop some of the other currencies — about being liked, wanting to be accepted by his peers and avoiding rejection — and selling himself more cheaply to do that.

Wanting to avoid rejection was a big currency for Darren. If someone knocked back a proposal, it was like a stake through his heart and he thought 'Oh no, I've lost a client.' He has increased his rates, and normally in the first five minutes of a meeting with a prospect he says: 'If cost is your primary criteria for engaging people I can refer you on to some really good people because that's not me.' Mostly they respond positively to the challenge — no one wants to miss out on value — and paradoxically, Darren's conversion rate has increased since he upped his rate and went with that frame instead of worrying about how much money prospects had to spend.

These days he just says, 'Well, you guys can't really afford not to do this, but I don't know what's important to you and whether you prefer low cost or not, and I charge a lot of money.' He very rarely misses the mark these days.

The difference getting to black belt has made in his life

The obvious difference is choices. Darren gets to make choices these days that he didn't get to make when he was either employed or struggling in the lower belts. He gets to make choices around which clients he wants to work with, so he probably knocks back or refers on twice the amount of work that he takes on himself.

He also has greater choices in lifestyle. Darren had a lovely family holiday to Bali at Christmas-time in peak season, saying "Financially we can afford it, let's do it." Probably one of the biggest differences in black belt and beyond sounds a bit like Buzz Lightyear in the *Toy Story* film — Darren feels more valued. Particularly at the lower belts, it's sometimes hard to see your value. As you get higher, there is a snowball effect where the market believes your value more and you believe your value more and you feel more valued in the marketplace, and that's a wonderful feeling.

18.

Red Belt

Give me a lever long enough and a fulcrum
on which to place it, and I shall move the world.

— ARCHIMEDES

Red belt is the fifth level on the Thought Leaders Revenue Ladder — it's $50,000 a month or $600,000 a year. At red belt, your practice starts to incorporate some components of a traditional business. You start to leverage more off other people's time and leverage your own IP more effectively.

BELT	INCOME	FOCUS
5th Dan	$1,200,000	Distribution
4th Dan	$1,080,000	Capacity
3rd Dan	$960,000	Productivity
2nd Dan	$840,000	Engagement
Black Belt	$720,000	Investment
Red Belt	**$600,000**	**Leverage**
Blue Belt	$480,000	Positioning
Green Belt	$360,000	Activity
Yellow Belt	$240,000	Value
White Belt	$120,000	Decision

FOCUS: LEVERAGE

To grow your practice, to get it making a million dollars a year, you need to find a way to leverage your time and the money you can make. There are two objectives as you build your practice. The first is *dollars up* — how can you increase the revenue in your practice and move up the belts? The second is *days down* — how can you maintain your income while reducing the number of days you work to bring it in?

Up until red belt, the focus is only on increasing revenue. You suck it in, knuckle down, put your shoulder to the wheel, drink a nice warm cup of toughen-up and do what you need to do. At red belt we also start to focus on bringing your days down. That happens through leveraging your time and your IP more effectively, and leveraging other people's time, effort, markets and IP.

But don't do this *until* you get to red belt! The quickest way to kill the growth of your practice is to take on activities that are beyond your current level — just as the quickest way to hurt yourself in a martial art would be to take on a black belt if you are only a white belt.

It's a lesson Pete learned the hard way. He tried to franchise his coaching practice (a classic red-belt leverage move) when he was still a white belt. He spent a lot of time and money replicating a system that wasn't yet good enough to be replicated. He invested a year and the best part of $100,000 franchising his coaching model, a model that had only taken him to white belt. He sold five franchises, and, not surprisingly, not one of them got off the ground. Pete eventually bought them all back. An expensive lesson in not leveraging too early.

Leveraging your time requires a shift in mindset away from selling and delivering units of time. By finding ways to deliver less but with more return, you are leveraging your time even further. This might also involve changing the way you sell and pitch for work. Initially, white, yellow and green belts quite often pitch to lower or middle levels of management and need to justify their day fees. This is often due to the level and market that their IP may be targeted at and their lack of positioning as an expert in the market. The more effectively you are positioned as an expert, the more you deal with senior management and the more you can leverage the value of what you are offering. This is when a typical $3,000–$5,000 training day can turn into a $100,000 training program that may only involve six touch points, which could include one to two days of needs analysis, three days of training and two days of coaching. As an expert, people are less likely to question— or analyze — what the fee is per day and will focus more on the outcome or results that you can deliver.

FIVE THINGS TO DO AT RED BELT

1. Get other people delivering your IP

We said earlier that as the thought leader your job is to think, sell and deliver. In the famous 1970s television show *The A-Team*, the character B.A. Baracus (played by Mr. T) says quite profoundly, "Rules are like noses; they are made to be broken." Red belt is where you break the rules a bit, and leverage other people's thinking, selling and delivery.

The most obvious way to do this is to have other people deliver your thinking. There are lots of ways you can do this. The most formal way is through franchising. This involves creating a brand and a detailed system that a franchisee can follow to deliver your stuff. It's expensive to set up, and is highly structured and regulated. It's not our favorite model — in our experience the relationship between the franchisor and franchisee often sours, and often after time the franchisee doesn't have an experience of receiving value for the ongoing expense and can become resentful — or want to create their own IP.

Licensing others to use your IP is not so tight, and typically only involves how the material and the thinking is delivered, not the brand it has to be delivered under. We generally think this is a better model for thought leaders than franchising. A franchise is essentially creating a whole business, with ongoing marketing and support where as a license can be an ongoing revenue stream with not much extra work.

The third way to leverage is to have others present your IP under your brand. This is something that Scott has done successfully with his training company, The Learning Difference. He trains other trainers in his IP and has them deliver under his brand as a contractor for specific projects with specific clients. Essentially, the contractors are seen as extensions of Scott and, depending on the client or the audience, he can use others to deliver his material. This is similar to the more traditional business model. The key is to make sure you don't end up like a traditional small-business owner having to manage a bunch of staff, with no time for your IP and positioning. Also, to maintain your brand integrity, you must ensure that your contractors have the skills, ability and experience to deliver to the level that your clients expect — otherwise your message, and the client, could be lost!

2. Leverage other people's markets

A great way to get leverage and accelerate the growth of your practice is to partner with people who already have a relationship with your target market.

Debbie Roberts, a thought leader in Melbourne, Australia, provides a textbook example of how to do this. Debbie has been a bookkeeper for over 30 years, and has been working as a thought leader teaching other bookkeepers how to grow their bookkeeping businesses. She delivers her expertise through speaking and authoring. Debbie has packaged up all the systems, templates, procedures and resources that she has developed over the last decade in her business (authoring) and gives a distribution keynote address (speaking) where she sells her system from the back of the room.

A year after launching her system, Debbie partnered with Australia's largest bookkeeping network. They have close to 2,000 members and a list of over 15,000 bookkeepers, and are known and trusted in the industry. They now sponsor Debbie's events, and promote them to their members and their list.

It's tempting to do this much earlier than at red belt, but generally it won't work. Hypothetically, say you launch a new cluster mentoring CEOs in how to lead more effectively. You think it's a great program and so you approach the CEO Institute and ask them to partner you, and put you in front of their members. The answer you'll get is a 'no'. They won't risk their reputation by putting an unknown quantity with no track record in front of their people.

However, if you come back a couple of years later as a red belt, with your book, great testimonials, case studies, white papers and a swag of thrilled customers (including some members of the network you are trying to get access to), it's going to be a completely different story. Now you are not a risk, but an opportunity to provide value to their members and potentially an additional income stream for them.

Debbie didn't approach the bookkeeping network when she was starting out; she did the hard yards herself first. She spent a year running her own events, ironing out her processes, collecting testimonials, improving her collaterals and establishing a tribe of raving fans. At the end of that year she was at a blue-belt running rate, and had sold 60 of her systems. She then teamed up with the bookkeeping network, and sold her next 60 systems in six weeks. Of course she gave up a percentage of her sales revenue, but she was still a long way ahead. Great leverage, and perfectly timed to take her from a blue-belt running rate to black belt.

3. Leverage other people's IP

There are times when you come across a set of IP that is a perfect fit for your practice. Someone has given their professional life to putting together a body of work that fits with what you do like a hand and a glove. And the smart thing to do, rather than try to start your own thinking in that domain from scratch, is to leverage their IP.

Thought Leaders have put together the most comprehensive methodology in the market for helping experts commercialize their thinking and develop a thought leadership practice. This book captures the essence of one segment of that work. If you wanted to launch a cluster in your practice to help clever people be commercially smart — training and mentoring experts to package, sell and deliver their IP — you might consider leveraging the IP that the partners at Thought Leaders Global have spent a decade putting together. Instead of building your own raft of IP, you could become an accredited Thought Leaders Mentor, and use their IP. It's a good leverage move because it gives you a shortcut, and will help you get a new cluster up, running and profitable, much more quickly than if you had to start it on your own. There are countless other examples of how you can do this.

Again, this is tempting to do earlier. However, if you do this too early you run the risk of becoming a gun for hire, delivering other people's programs without ever commercializing your own IP and becoming a thought leader in your own right. At red belt, though, it could be the perfect move to get another cluster off the ground quickly and get you to black belt and beyond. It is good positioning to introduce someone else's world-class thinking sitting alongside your own world-class thinking.

4. Create products

Creating products is another great way to leverage what you know. This can range from the simple to the complex. A simple example is the *Black Belt Under the Microscope* CD series. As part of the preparation for the first edition of this book, we interviewed a number of black belts about their practices. We had some really cool conversations and learnt a lot about different journeys from white belt to black belt and beyond. So we created a CD series of the interviews, realizing that there was great value for thought leaders to have a black belt sitting with them in their car or on their iPod sharing insights rather than listening to talk-back radio.

At the other end of the spectrum you can find solutions like creating and selling a board game around your IP. Thought leader Geoff McDonald is a games guru and has a unique ability to design games. As Geoff says, "When we play games we get lost in the learning. And that's what makes them one of the most effective ways to present training. We think through concepts, apply them in the game and receive instant feedback. That's an ideal learning loop." If you can take the learning and deliver it through a board game that doesn't need you to be present and can be licensed to other trainers, you have achieved powerful leverage and the ultimate product — capturing your IP.

Looking for ways to leverage your position in the digital world is an important step in your thought leadership. People need to be able to find you and what you offer easily. Providing offerings online can generate interest and income without you being there. These product offerings can be free, or you can charge for them. Quite often many thought leaders will have a range of free offerings that add so much value that people want more insights and are willing to pay for the next level of information. It is up to you to find the right mix of products that fits your target market and their preferred method of getting new information from you.

Products could include:

- Audio presentation

- eBooks

- DVDs and CDs

- Books

- Training manuals

- Games

- Diagnostic tools

- Online memberships

- Webinar series

- Online learning programs

5. Engage the third member of your team

Red belt is often a good time to engage more support and add a third member to your team. This could be a personal assistant for your business manager, or a contracted virtual assistant, locally or offshore.

As previously mentioned, your role as the thought leader is to 'make up' — you make up everything in the practice. The IP, the packages, the pricing, etc. You do the thinking, selling and delivering. The business manager does the set-up — sets up the sales, the venues, the packages, etc. The PA does the cleanup — what's left.

Interestingly, in this model the PA isn't your assistant — they are the business manager's assistant.

When your revenue is at red belt, above $600,000 a year, you have the income to provide your business manager with a part-time personal assistant — to free up their capacity to manage your practice further.

Avril Henry

Avril Henry graduated from the University of Cape Town in Accounting and Economics, migrating to Australia in 1980 with two suitcases, $500 and a dream to live freely and make a difference. Over the past 30 years, Avril has used this dream to build an award-winning corporate career that has spanned senior roles in finance, IT, project management, change management and HR, across multiple industries and countries.

In 2003, Avril left the safety of her corporate position to launch her practice and become a highly successful and widely popular keynote speaker, author, and corporate motivator. Since then she has been a finalist in the 2005 *Sydney Business Review* Business Woman of the Year awards and has been honored in the 2009 and 2010 Australian *Who's Who of Women* as one of the most inspiring businesswomen and female leaders.

As author of *The Henry Report*, she has also made a positive impact in one of the most traditional organizations in Australia — the military. Avril completed a Ministerial Review for the Minister of Defense into recruitment and retention in the Army, Air Force, and Navy that was accepted by the Government in December 2006. Following the review, Avril was appointed as a strategic advisor to the Chief of Navy, and joined the Navy's People Committee — the only civilian on the committee.

Avril is the author of *Leadership Revelations: An Australian Perspective* and *The Who What When and Y of Generation Why?* Her latest business book is entitled *Inspiring Tomorrow's Leaders Today: Breaking Down Generational Barriers At Work*, and she has just published her first children's book.

Getting to white belt

Avril was in the fortunate position of being quite well known in the HR field already, and the year before she set up her own business she was voted one of the top five HR directors in Australia. She was able to say to people that she was now a keynote speaker speaking about topics that she was particularly passionate about — managing people, leadership to different generations, gender diversity, and change management. Avril could approach people who already knew her, knew of her, or had seen her do presentations, because she had been presenting for about six years already. And when she told people that she was now running her own practice and was delivering keynote speeches and workshops, people were willing to pay because she had strongly positioned herself in the marketplace. Within six months of going out on her own, she was earning over $10,000 a month.

Main challenges getting to black belt

Avril used to think that work–life balance meant you have to have time off on a regular basis to relax and recharge your batteries. But over the last five years she has shifted in her thinking, and what she now believes is that work–life balance means different things to different people depending on where they're at in their life cycle.

In hindsight, Avril wishes she had had a better work–life balance when her children were young and at school, especially primary school. She was a single mother working in investment banking and had to do really long hours. Avril was one of the only two women on the senior management team, so she felt she had to put in the time.

Successful strategies

In looking at her success, there are a number of areas that Avril has used to get to the success she has achieved. First, she always believes in delivering value. In seven years Avril has not had an unhappy client. She has always sought to understand what her clients want.

Second, Avril always tailors her material to the client and the industry. She always does her homework. If she is going to go and work, even for a one-hour keynote address for a construction company, she will have a look at their website, look at their values, and always have a briefing over the phone with them beforehand to make sure she understands their key messages. To complement this, she has also crafted some very good templates. Avril is an ex-project director, so she is very structured in the way she collects information.

As well as researching the specific company, Avril will also research what the key issues are for their industry. She consistently gets feedback from people who have heard her speak three, four, five or six times, saying that they have never heard exactly the same presentation twice. The core messages around leadership, or around diversity, or around communication, are always the same because that is what Avril wants to reinforce — but the information she puts around the core messages is always tailored to the client and their industry.

Advice to someone starting out
Avril has four key tips, given to her about two years before she set up her business.

Number one — know what it is that you want to do. Have a very clear view of what it is that you have to offer. Avril knew that she wanted to offer people HR advice through keynote speeches, workshops, educating people, coaching people and mentoring programs, which would enable her to deliver management and leadership capability in the people space and to create positive, inclusive work environments. Everything that Avril does, including things like branding and recruitment strategies, can all be linked back to those two key objectives: building management and leadership capability, and developing positive and inclusive work environments.

Number two — know who your target market is. Make sure you are clear about who you are trying to help. Rather than trying to work with everyone, focus on a number of topics or industries that you will specialize in. By positioning yourself with a particular market, you will be able to charge what you are worth and add even more value.

Number three — start setting up what Avril calls the 'administrivia' a good six months before leaving your regular job. Avril had actually done things like set up the company and create her business plan beforehand, so that when she actually launched her practice she had already been working on those things. People leave their jobs and then try to figure out what to do next. But Avril believes this can often take you six to twelve months to work out in your own head.

And number four — have enough money to pay bills and live on for twelve months. In that first year, you're not earning the same money. It took Avril three years to get back to making the money that she was earning in corporate life as a senior executive. So, you also need to have enough money to live on and pay your bills.

Finally, you have to enjoy the journey because sometimes the journey's not fun. Being a thought leader, being passionate about what you do, and building a successful business is like being on a roller coaster. You will have highs and you will have lows; but as Avril tells her coaching clients "After every low there is a high, and when you're on a high beware because there will be a low. It's how you deal with the highs and lows that will make you effective."

Main lessons along the journey

The first is to always love what you do. The day Avril stops loving what she does, she'll stop doing it. Avril believes passion is what draws us to want to continuously improve.

She also believes that people should not forget to regularly thank the people who've helped them build their business — your team members, your suppliers, your family (who often don't see you). Avril holds a Christmas party every year and invites all of her suppliers, without whom she wouldn't be able to do her jobs. This includes her IT people, publications people, accountants and her lawyers. Then, at the after-party, Avril always invites the family members of everyone who works with her directly, including her partner, as a way of saying thank you.

Another key strategy is to remember that without your clients, you wouldn't be in business. So when clients are demanding, remember that sometimes they're demanding because they're under pressure, and it's an opportunity for you to help them achieve their deadlines.

One more of Avril's key philosophies is not to work with people you won't enjoy working with, whether as clients or as employees. She has turned down work when somebody has been rude to her staff. She worked in corporate life and has worked with people like that, but she is not willing to have that in her practice, whether it's team members, clients or suppliers. For Avril, having her own practice allows her the freedom to choose which clients she wants to work with — and to enjoy the journey as a result.

19.

Black Belt

Put all good eggs in one basket
and then watch that basket.

— ANDREW CARNEGIE

Black belt is $60,000 a month, or $720,000 a year. It's a phenomenal achievement in a thought leadership practice, and one worth celebrating.

BELT	INCOME	FOCUS
5th Dan	$1,200,000	Distribution
4th Dan	$1,080,000	Capacity
3rd Dan	$960,000	Productivity
2nd Dan	$840,000	Engagement
Black Belt	**$720,000**	**Investment**
Red Belt	$600,000	Leverage
Blue Belt	$480,000	Positioning
Green Belt	$360,000	Activity
Yellow Belt	$240,000	Value
White Belt	$120,000	Decision

In martial arts, particularly in the West, a lot of people quit after getting their black belt. Black belt was the goal, and when they get there and cross it off their list and they stop training.

Seiichi Sugano Shihan, 8th *dan* master in aikido and the person who introduced aikido into Australia from Japan, had a different approach. He said that when you got your black belt, that was when you started training. Up until then you were just getting ready to start. This is a great way to think about your practice. Black belt doesn't mean you've made it — it just means you are starting the next phase of your practice, your learning and your journey.

There is another great martial arts concept that translates beautifully — that of a beginner's mind. Training in martial arts means practicing the same technique again and again and again ... for 50 years in some cases. One way to think about a technique that you have done thousands of times is that you already know it. Another approach is to bring a beginner's mind to your training. Try to look at the technique as though for the first time. Discover what else you can learn about the technique, your opponent or yourself, as you practice.

Similarly, with your thought leaders practice, while you position yourself as an expert, don't get too caught up in your own story of success. Keep bringing your beginner's mind to your work, stay humble, and keep learning.

From a commercial viewpoint, black belt also doesn't mean you have made it. Typically you would expect to sustain your black-belt practice for about 10 years before you are set-up financially, as long as you follow our recommendations in the ten-year plan chapter and don't create a black-belt lifestyle to go with your black-belt practice. So, if you have had your first black-belt month, or your first black-belt year, by all means celebrate — and then plan for another 10 years of the same.

FOCUS: INVESTMENT

The key to maintaining your practice at or above black belt is *investment* — now is the time to invest in your practice, and particularly in its most important asset: you!

Do this at a level that doesn't negatively affect your income or your wealth plan. This isn't the time to spend $500,000 renting your dream office with the water views, 'investing' in a wardrobe and car to reflect your new income, and spending a corporate-level marketing and PR budget on your practice. Invest wisely in the things that will give you a financial return and set you up to maintain and grow your practice while bringing your delivery days down.

FIVE THINGS TO DO AT BLACK BELT

1. Invest in your practice efficiency

At black belt it's time to review and re-invent your systems. Your practice now looks a lot different to how it did at white belt, and some of the things you did at white belt might not make sense any more, or, at least, not the way you did them.

Also, in having a bigger team you will need to ensure that the systems have evolved to allow more effective communication and clear action that can be taken by all. When you are on your own there is not a need for a lot of systems, as you would have been doing everything and storing how you did it in your head. At black belt level it's important to re-work these systems to allow them to be operated by others; and to allow these others to improve on the systems and help them influence you to use the new and improved versions!

For example, when getting started many white belts use a free conference-call facility such as Skype to host small teleconferences. While this made sense at white belt, by the time you reach red belt the money you are saving doesn't justify the reduced quality of the service. Also, you may want the better functionality of a system such as GoToMeeting that provides you with screen controls as well as the ability to record the web-call and post it later as a webinar (for more details: www.gotomeeting.com).

2. Train your competitors (this makes you the master)

Training and mentoring your competitors is a great way to leverage off their expertise and positioning. This goes against the traditional thinking that anyone else who speaks, trains, mentors, or coaches in your domain is a competitor. If there were only a couple of clients hiring a couple of people talking on a couple of messages, then this might be something to be afraid of. However, we have found that there are so many different clients looking for different thought leaders with different messages that this line of thinking is very limiting.

Imagine that you could assist others in a specific area that is your expertise. This allows them to improve their skills and capabilities — and further establishes you as a master and a reference in the industry. It will also put your name at the front of their minds if they have a client looking for someone with your skill-set. If they respect your message and your delivery, it makes it much easier for them to refer business to you — and to help establish you as the thought leader in that domain.

Matt has nailed this within the Australian speaking community — he has trained many of the leading non-celebrity speakers in Australia. That makes him the master and has elevated his status to that of an admired thought leader. It also allows him to leverage his expertise, as many people have a business opportunity they will bring to him to collaborate on (which we will go into more detail in the next belt level!)

A further advantage of this approach is that it will force you to refine and create new IP. If you are sharing and leveraging your ideas, others will often adapt them into their delivery (hopefully while attributing your models to you). This means that as your ideas enter the marketplace, they become more accepted and understood — and therefore more commonplace. That will keep you creating and evolving your message further, as you will have to continue to stay in front of the competition!

3. Invest in your professional development

When Pete completed his Masters in Business, he realized that he didn't want to stop focusing on his education simply because he didn't have the formal structure of a university. Having already attended the University of Melbourne, the University of Illinois and RMIT University he established the University of Pete. The University of Pete only has one student (you guessed it — Pete). Each year Pete sets his curriculum at the start of the year — what the things are that he wants to learn, what the courses are he wants to attend, and what the books are he wants to read. For example, his curriculum at the time of writing the first edition of this book included:

- Diploma of Financial Services (to support his financial independence cluster)

- Speaking training

- Final Cut Express video-editing software

- Nature photography course

- Ongoing mentoring from two different mentors

- Reading 52 books a year

Now is a good time to establish the University of You, and kick it off with an aggressive professional development program. What domains of your business do you want to pursue mastery in? What technology do you want to get better at? Which mentors or coaches would you love to work with? What could you learn that will help you create more revenue or more efficiency within your practice? What books do you want to read? What delivery modes do you want to pursue mastery in?

As a thought leader, you need to keep thinking and keep learning, and when you get to black belt this is a good time to ramp up the learning.

4. Do more work you love with people you enjoy

The dream for a successful thought leadership practice is to get paid great money doing work you love, with people you enjoy, the way you want. Now is the time to align yourself and your practice with this dream.

Up until blue belt you are not allowed to say no to paid work (if the rate is right). If somebody wants to pay you for something, even if it's outside the clusters you are focusing on, you say yes. Once you get to blue belt you can start to be more discerning and turn down the work that doesn't position you effectively or that you don't want to do.

Doing work you love is what makes your practice sustainable. It means that even when you are working hard, you are getting energized rather than drained. Domonique Bertolucci says this beautifully: "We actually just spend our time doing what we love. Money flows through our life, so sometimes we are getting paid to do what we love, and sometimes we pay to do what we love."

5. Crank up your clusters

Black-belt practitioners can now begin to focus on cranking two or three primary clusters up to earn $500,000 to $1 million each. Start to plan for the future by answering the question: 'If I made $500,000 each from only three clusters, what would I want to be doing and for whom?'

For example, Matt has been a consistent thought leader for more than a decade. He has three primary clusters:

1. He runs the Thought Leaders Business School program for infopreneurs.

2. He delivers a motivational leadership message at corporate conferences.

3. He runs Speakership programs for professional keynote speakers.

He will sometimes have other clusters on the go, but these three are his main focus and his main game is keeping them strong, full and pleasurable.

Now that you are black belt, it's time to get clear and focused.

Michael Henderson

Michael Henderson is a real-life 'Indiana Jones' who has been lost in the Sahara Desert and exposed to severe bouts of exotic diseases that jeopardized his life in the pursuit of studying native cultures. This is what Michael builds on as the corporate anthropologist when he works with CEOs and executives in developing strategies to improve their cultures. He is a thought leader in helping organizations gain superior business results through understanding, inspiring and championing their workplace culture and the tribes at work within them. He is acknowledged as a global expert in the field of workplace culture and has used his unique skills to achieve commercial success.

What is a corporate anthropologist?
The word corporate is (as we all know in the business world) a big business. The 'anthropology' bit is the study of humans — particularly the study of humans in community and company, or, in really simple terms, the study of human culture and tribes. Michael has taken his knowledge and experience around anthropology and cultures and applied it to the business world. He looks at organizations not so much as commercial enterprises but as tribes with rituals, power, belief systems, values, and influence over others, and uses those insights to help organizations understand the cultures they have created for themselves.

Getting to white belt
Michael started as a trainer. Initially this was around sales training, and then it evolved to be specialized in Neuro-Linguistic Programming. He had been working with organizations that had low staff engagement which they wanted to work on. He sent out some newsletters offering a 90-minute consultation for $1,500 — and it

didn't take Michael long to reach eight to ten of those a month and get to white belt.

Main challenges

Michael has observed that there are two things that happen when someone begins to start the white belt process. One is that you have great hope. You look at the opportunity, you look at some of the thought leaders who have gone before and see what they are doing, and it's very inspiring and creates a great sense of a compelling future of what is possible. That can be really positive, as it draws you on.

The second is that at the same time, you have great doubt. So there are these two dynamics playing out — great hope and opportunity, and potentially great doubt too. Michael's doubts were: *'Will people get what I'm sharing?'* and, *'Could something like corporate anthropology, which is such a new concept of businesses, make money?'* Especially during the early years, the process of managing that dynamic of hope and doubt was very challenging for him.

As Michael says, it sounds a bit ridiculous but he managed it by actually stopping believing in himself. You can have positive and negative beliefs, none of which are necessarily true. So instead of listening to either his positive beliefs — *'Yes I believe it's possible'* — or his negative beliefs — *'Oh gosh, is the business world going to really get what I'm on about?'* — he just dropped all of that. He decided to get on and do it and ignore his own beliefs, both positive and negative. Which literally meant that he'd be sitting in a taxi going off to a client meeting and have the thought: 'Maybe these guys are going to be too harsh on this concept' and he would just totally ignore it. Likewise, he'd be heading to a meeting feeling extremely confident that he was going to blow them away and he would ignore that belief as well, and live in the reality of the conversation rather than his perception of what could or might happen.

At the time, Michael wrote, "I've decided I am unbelievable" in his diary. It catches both sides of the dynamic he was playing with, which was: '*I can completely let go of anything I'm believing,*' and at the same time the positive side: '*I'm unbelievable — I have got a lot to offer and this is my time.*'

He adopted this as a mantra for about the first twelve months. Michael would say to himself, '*It doesn't matter what I believe, it's the conversation with the client that is going to determine whether this thing happens or not — my belief or non-belief is actually redundant.*'

Key strategies

Michael embraced the recommended approach of having 150 coffees with 150 people and just sharing the offer with them. He believed that whether they took it up or not was not his concern. Michael's job was to get out there and let as many people as possible know what was available for them, and to give them the opportunity to say yes or no. At the risk of being simplistic, just get out there and have the 150 conversations with no hidden agendas, no intent, and no drive. Have the conversation, explain what it's all about, and let the other person do what they want. Some say yes and some say no and some say later.

Advice to someone starting out

Michael's advice to someone starting out is to do the work. It's very easy to have the conversation of thought leadership rather than do the work of thought leadership. It is a combination of the thinking and the commercialization of that thinking that builds a practice. And the people who are successful are still thinking.

The other advice that Michael gives comes from his brother, an Olympic athlete. He has a wonderful phrase: "*Dreams don't come true, you do.*" You can sit there and dream about being a black belt or writing a book, delivering keynote speeches or running/facilitating mentoring sessions, but dreams aren't going to do it. You have actually got to *do* the work, and that takes complete commitment to the process.

The difference getting to black belt has made

Michael reflects that getting to black belt has given him greater financial flexibility, meaning he can pick and choose which work he wants to do. Michael has the luxury of choosing which clients he wants to be associated with and which ones he doesn't.

Unexpectedly, it's given Michael far more time to think and evolve his own thinking. His expectation was that once he got to black belt he'd be run off his feet. Of course that's not the case, because the layers that he worked through to get to black belt prepared him and equipped him and evolved him so when he got to black belt he was actually far better able to leverage his time, money, and relationships.

The second consequence of getting to black belt is that Michael, in his own words, has 'gotten over himself'. He genuinely reflects more on his customers' behalf now. He spends a lot of his time thinking about his customers and their situations. During his own time, Michael will reflect *'OK, so that meeting we had yesterday with the client, how can I best resolve that? Who can I refer to out of the Thought Leaders community who could address that better than I can?'*

Michael really values the opportunity to think more authentically and generously on behalf of his clients.

On being a black belt

Michael believes that somewhere along the line, Western society has gained a core belief that good work and worthwhile work don't go hand-in-hand with money. We even think that charitable work shouldn't be earning a profit — it should be in service. Michael doesn't buy into that belief.

Michael thinks that good work and financial reward can not only be a very happy marriage, but possibly a marriage made in heaven. By becoming a thought leader, he has been able to do more effective work for his customers as a result of having the dollars available to market himself more effectively, to position himself more effectively, and even to spend more and invest more into his delivery process and programs. His financial stability lets him enhance the tools and offerings he has on delivering, mentoring and training sessions that before he just could not afford to.

Michael thinks that the belief that good work and good income are polar opposites doesn't serve us well as thought leaders. He collapses those polarities and is completely committed to being the best person he can be in the various roles that he serves in his life: as a father, a husband, a thought leader and an anthropologist. Earning good money as a result of this also enables Michael to be a good father, a good anthropologist and a good thought leader at the same time.

There was a Canadian personal-development guru floating around in the 1980s called John Kehoe who had a keynote address published in a book called *Mind Power*. One of the quotes in that book was *"Your success will help many, many people; your failure is likely to help no one including yourself."* Michael has drawn on that quote regularly when he found the going was getting tough or when things weren't going as quickly or as easily as he would have hoped.

20.

Beyond Black Belt

Let's live now, thinking of seven generations
of children following us.

— Native American proverb

The Thought Leaders' definition of success is making $500,000 to $1,500,000 doing work you love with people you like the way you want. We've talked so far about getting to black belt — $720,000 a year. After some time at black belt — perhaps a week, perhaps a year — you experience a mindset shift that you'll maintain for the rest of your life. Once that happens, and you feel comfortable being a black belt, then you have a decision to make: what comes next?

Once you've got to the $720,000 mark you can stay there fairly comfortably with the positioning you've earned and the conviction that comes with possessing a black belt mindset. Pushing beyond a million, however, starts to require unsustainable exertion again unless you make some smart decisions.

So why go for more? Why push yourself beyond black belt?

This is a good question, and one you need to explore quite seriously. You do need to know your drivers for success. Often, the highly ambitious are making up for some lack in their childhood. Napoleon had something to prove. We don't want to get all deep and meaningful on you, but now that you have achieved black belt you get to choose again.

There are four strategic choices you can make from this point onwards.

1. Grow: more of the same, and work harder

Keep growing the practice turnover. Employ more support staff; leverage the IP delivery by certifying coaches and training trainers who can take the IP to places you are unwilling or unable to go — different countries with different languages being an obvious example. Continue to launch new clusters. Crank up your primary clusters. Take your practice to a million dollars of revenue and beyond.

2. Shift: change gears and work smarter

Go from transactional modes across the board to leverage modes, as discussed earlier. Don't just write books; create membership sites. Don't speak for a fee; sell from the platform. Explore every minute spent and increase the return on investment of your time.

3. Flip: take yourself out of the game and turn it on its head

Take a 180-degree turn in direction. Move away from being a practice and begin to build a business. Take your name off the door, build proprietary software systems, and start to employ a management team and consistent service delivery. You stop being a technician and basically systematize everything so that it becomes turnkey. You may want to do this on your whole practice, or simply on a portion of it.

4. Live: use your practice as an experience passport

Use your practice to create rich life experiences. Go from simply measuring turnover (make sure you keep it high, though) to beginning to collect experience points. This is about the tax-effective business trip with family in tow. It's about who you meet, what you do and becoming the envy of your neighborhood. Got an intellectual crush on Seth Godin? Book him to deliver a keynote address at your conference. Think Harvard would look pretty cool on your resume? Enroll in a Harvard Business School intensive program. Enjoy tropical locations? Buy a villa in Bali and facilitate executive retreats there. Want to become fluent in Spanish? Play the game of maintaining a black-belt practice while you're based in South America. Take out your bucket list, and start ticking things off.

You might want to blend these strategies, and create hybrid solutions for you and your practice. The Thought Leaders methodology we are stepping through in this book and the accompanying programs are as straightforward as we can make them. We help clever people be commercially smart by taking away the 'tinkering' on system. It starts as a color-by-numbers approach. Clever people are then free to explore the creative outlets and fulfillment around their thinking, without having to worry that they are going broke doing so. After a few years, however, you then get to explore how the system can be adapted to suit you more. The point is that once you have mastered the science of getting all this done, you can graduate and start to explore the art of creating the life you want around your success.

There are obviously more choices here than simply the four listed above, so thought leaders wanting to take the next step shouldn't feel limited by the scope of these suggestions.

FIVE THINGS TO DO BEYOND BLACK BELT

1. Engage your tribe

Is it time to turn your customers into a movement? To bring together the people you touch with your thought leadership and turn them into a tribe? In his book *Tribes*, Seth Godin argues that the best way to get your ideas out into the world and to effect substantial change is through your tribe: a group of people connected to each other, to a leader and to an idea.

Do you have an idea that could inspire a movement? To bring together a tribe? It doesn't have to be grandiose. Gandhi inspired a movement around the idea that the British should leave India. However, your movement could equally be about sharing ideas with other users of your favorite database to help everyone get more out of it.

We are tribal creatures: we evolved in tribes, and we love to belong. Engaging your tribe means providing the structures for your members to engage with each other and to belong to something.

2. Get productivity obsessed

In the red belt chapter, we talked about the focus shifting from being solely about getting your revenue up to including getting your days down. Beyond black belt, we want to get obsessed with this idea, and place a whole new value on your time.

If you are aiming for a revenue of one million dollars a year, working 40 weeks a year, five days a week, that means you have 200 days to generate your revenue. This works out to $5,000 a day, and about $600 an hour for every hour of your working life. That becomes your new productivity benchmark. If you spend 15 minutes trying to get something to print because your printer got jammed and then you couldn't work out how to open the back, that's $150 wasted. If it takes you an hour of unproductive time travelling to a meeting and back, that's $600 that it's cost you to have the meeting. If you spend 10 minutes driving around to save $5 on a parking meter, it's probably a false economy.

Of course, these numbers aren't actually real, and you shouldn't let them go to your head and become silly about it. This is just a useful way to think about your productivity in order to become more productive. Thought leaders who are consistently running million-dollar-plus practices are amazingly productive. They typically accomplish in a day what many would take a week to get done. They stack activities. Travel time isn't unproductive — it's when phone calls are made or books are written. Meetings happen around other programs and projects, and only if they are strategic and productive. Not all emails and phone calls get returned. Time is treated with a new reverence, and we want to squeeze all the juice out of every minute.

There are so many things you do at this stage that no longer serve you. Drop bad habits, look for smarter ways to do what you do. Review systems and obsess about better ways of doing what you do. Ask yourself at all times, 'Is this the best use of my time right now?' (And would I pay myself $600 an hour for it?)

3. Look at building more capacity

Obviously, a big part of using your time more productively is to build more capacity outside yourself. How can you get rid of non-core activities? Who can you outsource to? This could be local or offshore, highly skilled or administrative. It might mean engaging a better bookkeeper who is going to make your life easier, or a lawyer who will save your time reading through legal agreements. Or it could be a virtual assistant in Manila who can review all your LinkedIn contacts and provide you with a report.

It's also a good time to look at lifting your own capacity. What can you do to lift your own capacity? Do you need to spend a day with someone learning how to use all your IT stuff more effectively? Do you need an exercise program that will keep your energy up through-out the day? Is it time to revisit your nutrition program and eat in a way that supports your capacity? Does meditation build your capac-ity? What do you need to get back into what you stopped doing?

4. Obsess about distribution

You have great products and you are more than making ends meet. Who can you joint venture with that might be able to get more of you in front of more people. You may have self-published to this point; do you now need to publish through a major distributor? Is there a network of people and the head of that network who can help you reach more people more easily? Do you need to form a strategic alli-ance with a professional body or association to deliver your material more broadly?

It's also a great time to create profitable projects with people you'd love to work with. Think about doing work you love with people you like the way you want. Who would you love to work with? Is there someone you would love to run a program with? Write a book with? Who do you want to play with and who would it make sense to distribute your IP with or through?

5. Focus more on your legacy work

Now is the time to focus more on your legacy work. Stephen Covey says that we have four primary needs: to live, to love, to learn, and to leave a legacy. A legacy is beautifully defined as 'planting a tree under which you will never sit.' It's about focusing some time on things bigger than you, things that will continue long after you have gone.

Think about your vision for the planet. What is the difference you want to make to your communities, to your cause, or to the planet as a whole? What domains do you want to have an impact on? Do you want to help end hunger? Save endangered tigers?

Help disempowered women in the subcontinent? Work with drug addicts in your home city? Find a cure for Parkinson's disease? Fight human-rights abuses? Now is the time to put your resources towards that — money, time, energy and your network.

Peter Sheahan

Peter Sheahan has spent a decade teaching businesses how to flip their thinking and find opportunity where others cannot. He believes that the real money gets made in the cracks, and that the opportunity for mind-blowing success is all around us. The problem is that we get conditioned by our experience, blinded by our business models, and conned by the popular media to believe success is a product of the economic conditions.

Peter's success is driven by his ability to identify areas of untapped potential within organizations, develop the unique thought processes needed to profit from them, and then catalyze the key individuals to take the risks required to make it a reality. Clients consistently remark on the depth of his insight, the global nature of his business perspective and the comprehensive research he does into their industry, their organization, its model, and the current threats and opportunities they face.

Peter's fifth book *FL!P*, an international bestseller available in 25 countries, emphasizes the need for leaders to have mindset flexibility. It explores the changing nature of leadership, evolving business models, and unpacks dozens of strategies for finding opportunity and making money in tough economic times. Peter walks his talks, and can speak from personal experience. A former general manager of a $10 million hotel business, Peter has established himself as a highly successful entrepreneur. In addition to his world-renowned thought leadership practice, Peter is also the CEO of Karrikins Group (formerly ChangeLabs). Karrikins Group specializes in large-scale behavior-change projects and now runs the largest face-to-face financial literacy program for teenagers in the world. In partnership with Apple, Karrikins Group developed and continues to run the groundbreaking Beyond Chalk program, working with educators to create 21ˢᵗ-century learning environments. Karrikins Group now has over 120 staff in 24 cities across 7 countries focusing on business growth and community investment programs in large corporations and government departments teaching staff how to use technology to foster collaboration and drive productivity in their organizations.

Peter's outstanding achievements were first officially recognized in 2003 when he had the honor of being named Young Entrepreneur of the Year in his home state of New South Wales, Australia. He is best known, though, for his skills as a presenter and his ability to customize his expertise to meet the needs of his audience. He has delivered more than 2,500 presentations to over 500,000 people in 20 different countries — most of these before the age of 30! In 2006, Peter was awarded the National Speakers Association Keynote Speaker of the Year award and is the youngest person to ever be inducted into their industry Hall of Fame in 2012.

Getting to white belt

Peter cold-called his way to his first $10,000 a month. He was speaking in high schools, so he had to do a lot of cold calling to get to white belt. The kind of volume you have to do in that market to get to $120,000 a year takes some pretty serious work. Peter had a fairly rough first six months, but in the first 18 he managed to get to white belt, and he did it with pure tenacity and persistence.

For the first four years of Peter's practice, his only modes were speaker and author. He published books but the money came from speaking.

Successful strategies going from white belt to black belt

From Peter's perspective, his success came down to five things.

Number one was quality on the platform. Peter went black belt on speaking fees, not on selling products at the back of the room and similar things. Ninety-five per cent of his income came from fee-for-service for delivering keynote speeches on the platform. It came down to just being really good at doing that.

Number two was positioning — having a topic which was in an area that was hot, and becoming synonymous with that topic. In Peter's case this was generational change. Ironically, in order to do this, you need to do one of two things: either work with a topic that no one's ever done before, which means it's completely unproven, or persist and publish like crazy in an area that is already well-recognized.

Peter did both. He published credibly, but he did it in an area that no one had yet played in. He was told by distribution partners like bureaus and agencies, and by publishers, that Gen Y was a very narrow area and no one was really that interested in it. Peter proved this not to be the case. He very quickly got positioning with a hot topic, much more quickly than he would have if he had tried to position himself where he is today in the area of behavior change in innovation.

Number three was publishing — not publishing to make money, but publishing for positioning. Peter now has six books published, and every 18–24 months he publishes a new book. Being an established author positions him in the marketplace as a person of authority — not to mention further positioning his value as a speaker.

Number four was doing the work. Peter works like crazy to nurture relationships with distribution partners. Once you get to a certain fee level most of the work goes through agencies, particularly overseas. It's a little different in Australia, but even if you want to go to that $10,000–$12,000 per presentation mark in Australia, those kinds of fees are generally for reasonably large events predominantly managed through a bureau or an agency relationship of some description.

For example, if a bureau puts a hold on an event for Peter for a software company, within 24 hours — no matter where he is in the world or how busy he is — he is going to respond to that hold with the list of experience he's got in the software space, and he'll send them a testimonial from Cisco, from SAP, from Mercury and from HP — people that they relate to. And then he'll send them his views of the software business right now and the move to software as a service, and he'll make some commentary about what's happening in the marketplace.

Peter will then add to that email his thoughts on the specific business, just based on looking at their press reel, what are they saying on their website, and what their CEO said in their most recent market update to analysts on Wall Street or the ASX. Then the bureau just falls over themselves with the work Peter has done and the value he has delivered. They send it on to the client, which gives them a great excuse to be back in touch — and all of a sudden Peter gets raised to the top of the list.

Finally, he always provided exceptional value. Peter will research like crazy before he does a presentation. The number one piece of feedback Peter gets for his work is around customization and research. So don't hire a marketing person — hire a research person. Peter finds that the research makes his presentations so good that they begin to market themselves.

Biggest mistakes

Peter's biggest mistake was doing a public seminar far too early and, as Peter says, 'sucking'. That was a pretty big mistake. He accepted briefs from clients that he knew he couldn't deliver on, and then under-delivered on platforms with 7,000 people.

Peter did a Million-Dollar Round Table — "Not my finest 20 minutes, let me tell you." This makes bureaus quiver, because they know that's the number one sales opportunity on earth. Peter let the client dictate the content, and he paid the price. He was too willing and excited about the opportunity, so he failed to properly position expectations with the client and set it up to win.

Peter also believes he could have done a better job at positioning product and extra value. Contrary to appearances, Peter is not the most confident guy in the world and he finds it very hard to stand on the stage and say: "You should really buy my book, it'll be good for you." Despite his success, he hasn't had the self-belief around some of his content and publishing, and consequently he's left a lot of money on the table.

Forget money — Peter has left a lot of *impact* on the table because he forgot just how much he wanted the next step. Peter draws a parallel with the Thought Leaders programs — if that had not been positioned in a meeting and if Peter had not signed up, he would not have gone black belt and beyond nearly as quickly as he did. He doesn't consider this as selling, but that he was given an opportunity. Peter has failed to give that opportunity to other people and he believes it has cost him a lot of money, it's cost a lot of brand equity, it's cost a lot of opportunity, and it's definitely cost a lot of impact.

Advice to someone starting out
Peter's key piece of advice is: "shut up and do the work." Not the updating your Facebook status kind of work. Doing the proper work — doing the research, developing the relationships. He cites another professional speaker, Patricia Fripp, as giving very sound advice — that the best marketing material you can have is a great presentation. So, do the work.

Second, be prepared to throw away what works. Garry Kasparov, the world chess champion, talks about the gravity of success — about how we get anchored to a certain way of doing things, anchored to a certain belief system, or comfortable in a level of success that robs us of the ability to get to the next level. Peter believes that breaking free of this gravity of success is what really makes a business an extraordinary business.

It's the willingness to just keep breaking free of your belief systems, keep breaking free of your work habits and your disciplines, and keep breaking free of even your own fears about what you think you're worth and what you think you can charge. Peter Sheahan is a great example of a thought leader who has taken this approach to reach black belt and beyond.

Next Steps

The late Charlie 'Tremendous' Jones is famous for saying that the key ingredients to success are the books you read and the people you meet. We think that you need to add a little resourcefulness as well.

Now that you've read the book, we'd like to extend an invitation to you to connect with us virtually. We've recorded a video implementation series which takes the lessons you've learned in these pages and helps you to apply them to your world. Our great hope is that reading this book is not simply an academic experience for you. We hope it is either the catalyst you need to effect massive change in your life or perhaps — for those of you who have been on the brink of making the change for a while — simply the straw that breaks the camel's back and puts you into action.

If change is what you seek, then implementation is imperative. The video series we've created is designed to help you to overcome inertia and get into momentum. It will help you identify the next steps in the path to developing your own thought leadership and building your black belt practice.

You'll find the free program at thoughtleaderspractice.com.

Thought Leaders Business School

Thought Leaders Business School is our flagship program. It runs in Australia and the USA. It is kind of like an MBA for thought leaders.

The world of education is experiencing a revolution. Lead by innovators like Khan Academy founder Salman Khan, many education experts are finding that the most effective learning programs 'flip the classroom'. This means the content is delivered to the students through online videos while they're at home, and the "homework" is done in class with the assistance of the teacher!

The benefit of this is that every student can learn at their own pace, in their own time. Concepts they find easy they can move through quickly. Material they find more difficult can be watched multiple times until it sinks in.

We've wholeheartedly embraced this concept at Thought Leaders, which means the entire curriculum of the Thought Leaders Business School program is available online. Featuring hundreds of videos, exercises, workbooks and collateral materials, the curriculum includes absolutely everything you need to develop your expertise into a black belt thought leaders practice.

It can be accessed from wherever you are in the world, at any time, and includes access to a tribe of like-minded experts all on a journey similar to yours.

One half of the proven-effective 'flipped classroom' model is the online delivery of the learning materials to the student. The other half is the guidance from a teacher/mentor to the student to help them implement what they've learned and successfully apply it in real life.

Thought Leaders Business School is the program we designed to massively shorten the time it takes to climb the revenue ladder and reach black belt. It provides everything you need to turn the theory of a commercially successful thought leadership practice into reality. Students are given the framework, sequence, accountability and support they need to:

- Focus on their thought leadership

- Develop, capture and package world class IP

- Develop clusters to take that IP to market

- Position themselves as the expert in their field

Thought leadership can be a lonely pursuit. In a practice, you'll generally be working alone, or with the help of just one or two staff, without the day-to-day support and interaction of a normal office environment (just a small price to pay to avoid the pointless meetings, perhaps!). Thought Leaders Business School provides an environment for you to thrive in. With the support of your personal mentor, and a community of inspiring thought leaders with an incredible diversity of experience and expertise, you will have access to everything you need to turn your ideas into commercial success.

Check it out at tlbusinessschool.com.

About the Authors

Matt Church

matt@mattchurch.com

Matt is the founder of Thought Leaders Global. He is a leading thinker who spends his time assisting others to raise the quality of their leadership in three key areas: Thought Leadership, Speakership and Motivational Leadership. An innovative entrepreneur, best-selling author and world-class conference speaker, he was recently recognized by the international speaking community as one of the 25 most influential people in the global speaking profession. He has been inducted into the Australian Speaker Hall of Fame, was 2014 Australian Speaker of the year, and E-speakers in 2015 rated Matt as one of the Top 10 Motivational speakers globally. A prolific author, he has published 11 books to date.

Peter Cook

peter@petercook.com

Thought Leaders CEO Peter Cook has built his business around teaching people how to leverage their expertise commercially. Peter has a passion for progress and an obsession with implementation. He is driven to help people be well rewarded, while doing work they love they with people they like the way they want. Peter is a best selling author with six books to his name, and another two on the way. These include *Implement!* and *The E-Myth Bookkeeper* which he co-authored with Michael Gerber. With over 15 years experience as a consultant to some of the biggest companies in the world, Peter is well-equipped to help thought leaders, business leaders and every day people achieve business and financial mastery.

Scott Stein

scott@scottstein.com.au

Scott works at a strategic level with individuals, leaders and business owners across Asia-Pacific and the United States to help them focus on what matters. He specializes in improving commercial advantage as well as advising on the best way to map the touchpoints required to reach success. He is an author of three books and is a Thought Leaders Global Partner whilst also running two successful business practices and a property trust. Born in the United States and currently based in Australia, Scott has a master's degree in communication and has worked as a speaker, trainer, mentor, facilitator, coach and change agent with many of the top national and international organizations over the past 25 years.